D1709961

GIDEON

▬▬▬ V. ▬▬▬

WAINWRIGHT

The Right to

Free Legal Counsel

GREAT SUPREME COURT DECISIONS

Brown v. Board of Education
Dred Scott v. Sandford
Engel v. Vitale
Furman v. Georgia
Gideon v. Wainwright
McCulloch v. Maryland
Marbury v. Madison
Miranda v. Arizona
Plessy v. Ferguson
Regents of the University of California v. Bakke
Roe v. Wade
United States v. Nixon

Great Supreme Court Decisions

GIDEON
━━ V. ━━
WAINWRIGHT

The Right to

Free Legal Counsel

G.S. Prentzas

CHELSEA HOUSE
PUBLISHERS
An imprint of Infobase Publishing

In memory of Craig Haltom

Gideon v. Wainwright

Copyright © 2007 by Infobase Publishing

Chelsea House
An imprint of Infobase Publishing
132 West 31st Street
New York, NY 10001

ISBN-10: 0-7910-9383-2
ISBN-13: 978-0-7910-9383-2

Library of Congress Cataloging-in-Publication Data
Prentzas, G. S.
  Gideon v. Wainwright : the right to free legal counsel / G.S. Prentzas.
    p. cm. — (Great Supreme Court decisions)
  Includes bibliographical references and index.
  ISBN 0-7910-9383-2 (hardcover)
  1. Gideon, Clarence Earl—Trials, litigation, etc.—Juvenile literature. 2. Wainwright, Louie L.—Trials, litigation, etc.—Juvenile literature. 3. Right to counsel—United States—Juvenile literature. 4. United States. Supreme Court—Juvenile literature. 5. Right to counsel. I. Title. II. Series.
  KF228.G53P74 2007
  345.73'056—dc22   2006023241

Chelsea House books are available at special discounts when purchased in bulk quantities for businesses, associations, institutions, or sales promotions. Please call our Special Sales Department in New York at (212) 967-8800 or (800) 322-8755.

You can find Chelsea House on the World Wide Web at http://www.chelseahouse.com

Text design by Erika K. Arroyo
Cover design by Takeshi Takehashi

Printed in the United States of America
Bang EJB 10 9 8 7 6 5 4 3 2 1

This book is printed on acid-free paper.

All links and Web addresses were checked and verified to be correct at the time of publication. Because of the dynamic nature of the Web, some addresses and links may have changed since publication and may no longer be valid.

EQUAL·JUSTICE·UNDER·LAW·

Contents

EQUAL·JUSTICE·UNDER·LAW·

Introduction

On January 8, 1962, the U.S. Supreme Court received a large brown envelope from Clarence Earl Gideon. A lifelong drifter and career petty thief, the 51-year-old inmate was serving a five-year sentence for a break-in. The envelope contained a petition asking the nation's highest court to review his case.

Gideon claimed that he had been denied due process of law at his trial in Florida. The Fourteenth Amendment to the U.S. Constitution, he noted, guarantees that no state shall take any citizen's "life, liberty, or property without due process of law."[1] At his trial, Gideon had asked the judge to provide him an attorney to assist in his defense. Following state law, the judge had denied the request. In his petition to the Supreme Court, Gideon insisted that he was imprisoned illegally. He claimed that the due process clause of the Fourteenth Amendment required the State of Florida to provide him a lawyer. Gideon also asserted that the state should have offered an attorney free of charge because he could not afford to hire one.

The secretary who opened the envelope sent Gideon's petition to a Court clerk. The clerk checked to make sure that it met the Court's rules for filing an appeal. Under Court rules, criminal cases like Gideon's must be appealed within 90 days of a lower court's decision. Gideon had petitioned the Florida Supreme Court, seeking a writ of *habeas corpus*. (This is the Latin phrase for "you have the body.") A writ of habeas corpus is an order issued by a court. It requires a prison official to bring an inmate before the court so it can decide whether the person is imprisoned lawfully. Gideon had enclosed a document showing that the Florida Supreme Court had rejected his request for a writ of habeas corpus on October 30, 1961. Thus, he had satisfied the 90-day requirement.

Gideon's petition also included a motion to proceed *in forma pauperis* (Latin for "in the form of a poor person"). Under Supreme Court rules, poor people can file an appeal without paying the usual filing fees. The Court normally requires appeal petitions to be printed. *In forma pauperis* petitions, however, can be typed or handwritten. Gideon's seven-page petition was handwritten in pencil on sheets of paper provided by the Florida prison system.

Gideon had followed all of the Court's rules. The clerk assigned his case a number: 890 Miscellaneous. This meant that it was the eight hundred ninetieth case on the Court's Miscellaneous docket. The Miscellaneous docket is a group of cases consisting mostly of petitions from convicts seeking their release from jail. As his case number indicated, Gideon was merely one of many prisoners asking the Supreme Court to review their case. The Court received eight other *in forma pauperis* petitions from inmates on the same day that Gideon's envelope arrived. The clerk also gave the case a formal name, *Gideon v. Cochran*. (The *v.* in the names of legal cases is an abbreviation for *versus*, or against.) It identified the case's two parties: Clarence Earl Gideon and H.G. Cochran, Jr. Cochran was the director of Florida's prisons. The case name would later be changed to *Gideon v. Wainwright*, when Louie L. Wainwright replaced Cochran. The clerk then sent Gideon's paperwork to the file room. It would remain there until the Court acted on his petition.

A FEDERAL CASE

The U.S. Supreme Court does not have the power to review all cases. It has limited jurisdiction. Jurisdiction is the legal term for the scope of a court's authority to hear cases. The U.S. Constitution, laws passed by Congress, and rules set by the Court itself restrict the types of cases the Supreme Court can review. Article III of the Constitution describes the types of cases that can go directly to the Supreme Court. These include cases concerning treaties with other countries and lawsuits involving two states. These types of cases are rare, however.

Most Supreme Court cases involve an appeal of a lower court's decision. Under the Judiciary Act of 1789, the U.S. Supreme Court can review all rulings made by federal courts. It can also review rulings by state courts concerning federal law. The Court, however, cannot review any ruling made by a state court concerning a state law. The highest court in each state has the final say about the meaning and application of the laws of its state. Most legal cases are tried in state courts and involve state laws. These include criminal trials and personal and business lawsuits. Thus, the Court has the power to review only a relatively small percentage of cases decided throughout the country.

Gideon had to overcome several obstacles in order to have the Supreme Court hear his case. First, he had to show that the Court had jurisdiction. Because his case presented a constitutional question—whether the trial court had violated his Fourteenth Amendment rights by refusing to provide him counsel—Gideon met this requirement.

The U.S. Supreme Court building houses the highest court in the country. The Court's responsibility is to ensure a high standard of justice for all Americans by deciding important cases such as *Gideon v. Wainwright*.

Gideon's next hurdle was much higher. In 1925, Congress gave the Court the power to select only the most important cases to review. Thus, anyone seeking a Supreme Court appeal must convince the Court that his or her case is particularly important. If four of the Court's nine justices agree that a case presents an important legal issue, the Court will issue a writ of *certiorari* (pronounced *sursh-ee-o-rar-ee,* from the Latin word meaning "to be informed.") It is a formal order that allows the case to be brought up from a lower court for consideration. If the Court denies a petition of certiorari, then the decision of the lower court is final.

The Court receives many more appeals than it can possibly hear. Current Supreme Court rules state that a "[r]eview on a writ of certiorari is not a matter of right, but of judicial discretion. A petition for a writ of certiorari will be granted only for compelling reasons."[2] (Currently, the U.S. Supreme Court receives between 5,000 and 8,000 appeals each year. Of these, the Court agrees to hear about 80 to 100 cases.) At the time of the *Gideon* case, the Court received about 2,500 appeals a year and agreed to hear about 150 each year. The odds seemed very slim that the Supreme Court would grant a writ of certiorari based on a handwritten petition from a poorly educated prisoner like Gideon.

Finally, Gideon faced another problem in convincing the Court to hear his case. At his trial, Gideon had stated, "The United States Supreme Court says I am entitled to be represented by counsel."[3] He based his petition to the Supreme Court on this claim. Gideon's understanding of the law, however, was completely wrong. Twenty years earlier, in *Betts v. Brady* (1942), the Court had ruled that the U.S. Constitution did not require states to provide court-appointed counsel for criminal defendants. Unknowingly, Clarence Earl Gideon was boldly asking the Supreme Court to change its mind and change the law.

THE COURT CONSIDERS GIDEON'S PETITION

On February 8, 1962, a clerk sent Gideon's file to the office of Chief Justice Earl Warren. The chief justice's law clerks review all *in forma pauperis* petitions. (Supreme Court law clerks are recent law school graduates who help the nine justices research and write their opinions.) The clerks prepare a summary for each *in forma pauperis* case. They then circulate the summaries to all the justices.

After reviewing the summary of Gideon's case, the justices discussed his petition during a conference held on Friday, June 1, 1962. These Court conferences are held in strict secrecy, so there is no record of the justices' conversation. On the following Monday, June 4, the Court's orders from their Friday conference were posted. The order concerning Gideon's petition read:

> The motion for leave to proceed in forma pauperis and the petition for writ of certiorari are granted. In addition to other questions presented by this case, counsel are requested to discuss the following in their briefs and oral argument: Should this Court's holding in *Betts v. Brady* be reconsidered?[4]

Even though Gideon's handwritten petition was riddled with misspellings, misinterpreted the law, and showed a lack of legal training, the Supreme Court had agreed to hear his case. A felon, handling his own appeal from his Florida jail cell, had convinced the nation's highest court that his case was important.

1

The Making of a Landmark Case

Clarence Earl Gideon was happy to hear that the U.S. Supreme Court had agreed to review his case. Finally, someone in power was listening to him. Gideon also found out that the Court had appointed a lawyer to represent him. Whenever the Supreme Court agrees to review the case of a poor petitioner, it appoints a lawyer to argue the case. The justices had met at their weekly conference on June 22, 1962. They discussed the appointment of a lawyer to handle Gideon's case. After the conference, Chief Justice Warren instructed a clerk to notify Abe Fortas that he had been selected to represent Gideon. Fortas was an experienced and widely respected Washington, D.C., attorney with an interest in the rights of the accused. After hearing a brief description of the case, Fortas quickly agreed to represent the Florida prisoner who had been denied a lawyer at his trial.

THE LIFE OF A DRIFTER

Abe Fortas read through the court documents on Gideon's case. In order to build the strongest case possible for his new client, he needed more information. He wrote Gideon a letter, asking for details about his life and the trial. In a letter to Fortas, Gideon recounted his life story.

Gideon was born on August 30, 1910, in Hannibal, Missouri. His father died when he was three years old. His mother soon remarried, but Clarence never got along with his stepfather. At age 14, he dropped out of school and ran away from home. To cope with cold weather, he shoplifted some clothes from a small country store. He was arrested when the store's owner spotted him wearing the missing garments. A juvenile court in Ralls County, Missouri, sentenced him to a reformatory for three years. Gideon later recalled, "[Of] all the prisons I have been in that was the worst. I still have scars on my body from the whippings I received there."[5] Released after spending one year in the reformatory, the 16-year-old found work in a shoe factory. Two years later, he lost his job. He was soon in jail again, sentenced to 10 years for robbery. After serving 4 years, Gideon was paroled (released early). He left prison only to find the nation's economy struggling. The U.S. stock market had crashed three years earlier, in 1929, wiping out many businesses. At the lowest point of this economic crisis, known as the Great Depression (1929–1941), more than 16 million people were unemployed. That was about one-third of the country's labor force.

It was particularly hard for an ex-convict to get a job. Gideon could find only occasional work, so he once again resorted to petty crimes. In 1934, he was caught stealing government property from an armory. A federal court sentenced him to three years in the federal prison at Fort Leavenworth, Kansas. Released after serving two years, Gideon was in and out of jail over the next few years. In 1940, he escaped from a Missouri prison and assumed the name Barney Smith. He worked as a railroad brakeman for several years. His mug shot, however, appeared in *True Detective*, a popular crime magazine. A reader recognized Gideon and turned him in as a fugitive. He soon found himself back behind bars.

This revolving-door pattern continued until 1952, when Gideon was released from a Texas prison after serving a year for yet another robbery. He settled down in Orange, Texas. He worked at various jobs, including tugboat cook and fisherman. This time, he managed to stay out of trouble with the law. Gideon saved enough money to buy a bar and pool hall. It seemed that he had finally gotten his life together. Things took a turn for the worse, however. In 1953, he was stricken with tuberculosis, a serious disease that affects the lungs. He had several long stays in hospitals during the next few years.

Gideon had married four times. His relationship with his current wife, Ruth, was stable. They had three children together. The Gideon family moved to Panama City, Florida, in 1958. Clarence found work as an auto mechanic, but the pay was low. To make a little extra money, he often gambled. He joined poker games wherever he could find them.

On June 3, 1961, the Panama City police arrested Gideon for an early-morning break-in at a Panama City pool hall. The vending machine coin boxes at the crime scene had been emptied; an eyewitness had pointed Gideon out as the burglar. When police found him in a downtown bar, $25.28 in coins weighed down Gideon's pants. The police were convinced that they had their perpetrator. Gideon, however, denied any involvement in the break-in. He insisted that the coins in his pockets were his winnings from a low-stakes poker game.

Clarence Earl Gideon, photographed in 1961, fought to obtain legal counsel for all defendants charged in state cases.

GIDEON'S TRIAL

In his letter to Fortas, Gideon also described his trial on the burglary charges. On August 4, 1961, Gideon had appeared for trial before Judge Robert L. McCrary, Jr., of the Circuit Court of the Fourteenth Judicial Circuit of Florida. He was formally charged with breaking and entering into the Bay Harbor Poolroom with the intent to commit larceny (theft).

Fortas also had access to additional information about the trial. A court reporter recorded the proceedings of Gideon's trial in a written document known as a transcript. The trial's transcript provided an account of a key conversation at the beginning of the trial:

> *The Court:* The next case on the docket is the case of the State of Florida, Plaintiff, versus Clarence Earl Gideon, Defendant. What says the State, are you ready to go to trial in this case?
>
> *Mr. Harris (William E. Harris, Assistant State Attorney):* The State is ready, your Honor.
>
> *The Court:* What says the Defendant? Are you ready to go to trial?
>
> *The Defendant:* I am not ready, your Honor.
>
> *The Court:* Did you plead not guilty to this charge by reason of insanity?
>
> *The Defendant:* No sir.
>
> *The Court:* Why aren't you ready?
>
> *The Defendant:* I have no counsel.
>
> *The Court:* Why do you not have counsel? Did you not know that your case was set for trial today?
>
> *The Defendant:* I have no counsel.
>
> *The Court:* Why, then, did you not secure counsel and be prepared to go to trial?

The Defendant: Your honor . . . I request this Court to appoint counsel to represent me in this trial.

The Court: Mr. Gideon, I'm sorry, but I cannot appoint counsel to represent you in this case. Under the laws of the State of Florida, the only time the court can appoint counsel to represent a Defendant is when the person is charged with a capital offense. I am sorry,

ABE FORTAS

Abe Fortas (1910–1982) was born in Memphis, Tennessee, the same year as Clarence Earl Gideon. He graduated from Southwestern College (now Rhodes College) and Yale Law School. For nine years, he taught courses at Yale Law School while working at various federal government jobs in Washington, D.C. In 1942, President Franklin Roosevelt appointed him undersecretary of the Interior, the executive branch department that manages most federally owned land. In 1946, Fortas left the government and co-founded a law firm in the nation's capital. His legal expertise and trial skills soon earned him much respect in the legal community. He represented the defendant in *Durham v. United States*, an important 1954 case that broadened the legal definition of insanity in criminal cases. In 1963, the Supreme Court appointed him to represent Clarence Earl Gideon.

In 1965, President Lyndon B. Johnson, a close friend, appointed Fortas to succeed Arthur Goldberg on the Supreme Court. As an associate justice, he supported the Warren Court's efforts to expand civil rights, including those of people accused of crimes. In 1968, Johnson nominated Fortas as chief justice when Earl Warren stepped down. Some senators opposed his nomination, however. Fortas eventually withdrew his nomination. The following year, Fortas became embroiled in an ethics controversy and resigned from the Court under public pressure.

but I will have to deny your request to appoint counsel to defend you in this case.

The Defendant: The United States Supreme Court says I am entitled to be represented by counsel.

The Court: Let the record show that the defendant has asked the court to appoint counsel to represent him in this trial and the court denied the request and informed the defendant that the only time the court could appoint counsel to represent a defendant was in cases where the defendant was charged with a capital offense. The defendant stated to the court that the United States Supreme Court said he was entitled to it.[6]

The transcript showed that Gideon and Harris made their opening remarks to the jury. Then, William Harris, the prosecutor, presented the state's witnesses. The prosecution's key witness was Henry Cook. The 22-year-old testified that he was standing outside the Bay Harbor Poolroom at 5:30 A.M. on June 3, 1961. He claimed that he saw Gideon inside the pool hall. According to Cook, Gideon later exited the building holding a bottle of wine. He made a call at the telephone booth on the corner. A taxi arrived a few minutes later, and Gideon hopped inside. Cook ended his testimony by saying that he looked into the pool hall again and saw that it "had been broken into."[7]

Gideon then had his chance to cross-examine the witness. He asked Cook several questions that did not appear particularly relevant. He then asked Cook a seemingly important question: Why was he standing around outside the pool hall so early in the morning? Cook replied that he had "just came from a dance down in Apalachicola, stayed out all night."[8] Gideon didn't follow up with any other questions.

Next, the owner of the pool hall, Ira Strickland, Jr., testified for the prosecution. He told the court that when he arrived at

Gideon's appeal was heard by the Florida Supreme Court before eventually climbing to the U.S. Supreme Court.

work that morning, he discovered a broken window. Inside, someone had forced open the cash boxes of the cigarette machine and jukebox. The coins from both machines were missing. He didn't know the amount. The burglar also took some beer and wine. After Strickland's testimony, the prosecution rested its case.

Gideon called eight witnesses on his behalf. The first was Henry Berryhill, Jr., the police officer who had discovered the break-in. He testified that he noticed the pool hall's front door was open. He "checked with a fellow at the front of the building, a Mr. Cook, and he said he saw you [Gideon] leave the building."[9] Gideon's other witnesses included a deputy sheriff who had investigated the crime, the taxi driver who had picked up Gideon that morning, and several people from the neighborhood. The questions that Gideon asked his witnesses did little to help establish his innocence.

The transcript showed that after both sides had presented their case, the judge gave instructions to the jury of six men. The jury left to deliberate the case and soon returned with a verdict: guilty. Judge McCrary delayed sentencing until he could review Gideon's criminal record. On August 27, McCrary gave Gideon the maximum sentence for breaking and entering: five years in prison.

"A FLAME STILL BURNED"

Gideon admitted that he had been a petty thief for much of his life, but he insisted that he was innocent of the Bay Harbor Poolroom burglary. "A flame still burned in Clarence Earl Gideon," journalist Anthony Lewis wrote in *Gideon's Trumpet*, a book that details Gideon's fight for the right to legal counsel. "He had not given up caring about life or freedom; he had not lost his sense of injustice. Right now he had a passionate—some thought almost irrational—feeling of having been wronged by the State of Florida, and he had the determination to try to do something about it."[10]

Once Gideon arrived at the state prison at Raiford, Florida, he tried to get the authorities to hear his plea that he was wrongly imprisoned. He wrote a letter to the Federal Bureau of Investigation (FBI) explaining his case. The FBI, which had no connection with Gideon's case, never replied. To learn how to appeal his conviction, he studied the old law books in the prison library. Gideon filed a petition for a writ of habeas corpus with the Florida Supreme Court. The court turned down the petition. Their order read: "The above-named petitioner has filed petition for writ of habeas corpus in the above cause, and upon consideration thereof, it is ordered that said petition be and the same is hereby denied."[11] The court did not

In The Supreme Court of The United States
Washington D.C.
Clarence Earl Gideon
        Petitioner   Petition for a writ
vs.   of Certiorari Directed
H.G. Cochran, Jr, as   to The Supreme Court
Director, Divisions   State of Florida.
of corrections state   No. 890 Misc.
of Florida   OCT. TERM 1961
                            U.S. Supreme Court
To. The Honorable Earl Warren, Chief
    Justice of the United States
        Comes now The petitioner, Clarence
Earl Gideon, a citizen of The United states
of America, in proper person, and appearing
as his own counsel. Who petitions this
Honorable Court for a Writ of Certiorari
directed to The Supreme Court of The State
of Florida. To review the order and Judge-
ment of the court below denying The
petitioner a writ of Habeus Corpus.
        Petitioner submits That The Supreme
Court of The United States has The authority
and jurisdiction to review The final Judge-
ment of The Supreme Court of The State
of Florida The highest court of The State
Under sec. 344 (B) Title 28 U.S.C.A. and
Because The "Due process clause" of th_

In a 1963 petition, Gideon charged that his Florida trial was
unjust because he was denied legal representation.

discuss the facts of Gideon's case or provide the reasons for their decision.

The Florida Supreme Court's ruling did not discourage Gideon. He went back to studying law books to learn how to appeal his case to the U.S. Supreme Court. On prison stationery, he carefully wrote out two petitions in pencil. One was a petition for a writ of certiorari, asking the Court to review his case. The other was an *in forma pauperis* petition, requesting the Court to waive certain filing fees (and other rules) because he could not afford to pay them. Gideon's spelling and grammar were not perfect, but he made his legal arguments plainly and clearly.

In his petition for writ of certiorari, Gideon summed up the grounds for his appeal:

> When at the time of the petitioner's trial he asked the lower court for the aid of counsel, the court refused this aid. Petitioner told the court that this Court had made decision to the effect that all citizens tried for a felony crime should have aid of counsel. The lower court ignored this plea.[12]

Gideon's petition captured the attention of a Supreme Court law clerk. He felt that this was a case that the Court may wish to review. He prepared a summary of the case for the justices.

Before circulating the summary and Gideon's file among the justices, the law clerk asked the Court clerk to send a letter to the State of Florida asking them to respond to Gideon's petition. This procedure gives state authorities an opportunity to comment on the legal issues involved in a case and to provide information not found in a prisoner's petition. On March 8, 1962, the Court clerk sent a letter to the attorney general of Florida, requesting comments on Gideon's petition.

The response from Florida's attorney general, Richard W. Ervin, arrived on April 9, 1962. He stressed that that the Court should not hear Gideon's case because he had not been entitled to legal counsel at his trial. Erwin pointed to the Court's decision in *Betts v. Brady* (1942). In that case, the Court had held that the Constitution did not guarantee free lawyers to all poor defendants tried for crimes in state courts. It had ruled that states were obligated to provide legal counsel to poor defendants only when special circumstances showed that a fair trial would otherwise be impossible. Later cases showed that these special circumstances included such factors as a very young defendant, a mentally challenged defendant, or a case in which racial discrimination could affect the outcome of the trial. Erwin argued that Gideon had not claimed any special circumstance required by the *Betts* rule. "Petitioner Gideon," his letter stated, "has made no affirmative showing of any exceptional circumstances which would entitle him to counsel under the Fourteenth Amendment."[13]

Following Court rules, Erwin had sent a copy of the letter to the petitioner. Gideon sent a brief letter to the Court responding to Erwin's arguments. He wrote, "It makes no difference how old I am or what color I am or what church I belong to. . . . The question is very simple. I requested the court to appoint me attorney and the court refused."[14] The Court clerk added the letters from Florida's attorney general and the petitioner to Gideon's file, which was then sent to the justices.

After reviewing Gideon's file and discussing his case, the Court granted a writ of certiorari. The Court soon appointed a lawyer to represent Gideon and set dates for various court filings. They also set a date for oral arguments, where the lawyers for each side would make their legal arguments and answer questions posed by the justices of the Supreme Court.

History of the Right to Counsel in the United States

2

I n preparing their arguments for *Gideon v. Wainwright*, the attorneys on both sides researched the history of the right to counsel (the right to have a lawyer) in the United States. Many of the basic laws and procedures of the U.S. legal system can be traced back to England. Parliament, England's legislative body, passed most of the laws that governed the country's colonies in North America. Courts and colonial officials in the original 13 colonies applied British laws and followed the criminal procedures of the British legal system.

In England, the right to a trial by a jury of one's peers had long been a right granted to criminal defendants. King John

(1167–1216) had signed the Magna Carta in 1215. This ground-breaking document limited the powers of the English monarchy. In addition to addressing the complaints of the British nobility, it set down the basic legal rights of all of the country's free men. Notably, the Magna Carta forbade taxation without representation and guaranteed the right to a jury trial.

England granted the right to counsel to persons accused of minor crimes, known as misdemeanors. Those accused of major crimes, known as felonies, however, had no right to counsel. Legal scholars believe that this seemingly odd system showed that the British government was willing to be more lenient in minor cases. Parliament passed a law in 1695 that allowed defendants to hire counsel in treason trials and required courts to appoint counsel on request. A person convicted of treason, a crime involving betraying one's country, would be executed. Parliament would not pass a law allowing the right to counsel in all felony cases until 1836. After 1750, however, many English judges began allowing counsel at felony trials as a matter of their own discretion.

Courts in the American colonies generally followed English legal practices and traditions. The reality of the American system, however, was that there were few trained lawyers in the colonies during the seventeenth and early eighteenth centuries. Private individuals often brought criminal charges. Courts were considered to be extensions of the colonial government. Defendants usually represented themselves. As the population in the colonies increased, the colonies' legal systems evolved. Judges began viewing themselves as neutral authorities. Public prosecutors, rather than private individuals, took over the role of pursuing criminal charges.

Pennsylvania was the only colony to provide for a general right to counsel. In 1701, William Penn, the proprietor of Pennsylvania, signed the Charter of Privileges. This document granted the citizens of his colony greater control over the government and broader civil liberties. Article V gave colonists accused of crimes the same right of counsel as the prosecution. The charter read, "All Criminals shall have the same Privileges of Witnesses and Council as their Prosecutors."[15] Courts in the other colonies allowed legal counsel on a case-by-case basis. As political tensions with England grew, colonists began to view the right to counsel as a basic safeguard of liberty.

THE CONSTITUTION AND THE RIGHT TO COUNSEL

Political and economic grievances in the British colonies led to the American Revolutionary War (1775–1783). After winning on the battlefield and gaining independence from England, the 13 states approved the Articles of Confederation (1781). This document was the first national constitution of the United States. Because of their experience with strict central authority under British rule, most Americans wanted the states to exercise the majority of governmental powers. The Articles of Confederation did not guarantee any fundamental rights. The delegates who drafted and approved the Articles of Confederation assumed that the states would provide for the rights of their citizens in their own constitutions.

The original 13 states recognized the right to counsel, either in their constitutions or by passing laws. The right to counsel was recognized in the constitutions of Maryland (1776), New York (1776), New Jersey (1777), Massachusetts (1780), and New Hampshire (1784). (The right to counsel would later be recognized in the constitutions of all the other original states, except Virginia and South Carolina.) Pennsylvania, Delaware, North Carolina, South Carolina, and Virginia enacted statutes that recognized the right of the accused to hire counsel. The other original states later passed similar laws.

In most cases, in constitutions or statutes, the right to counsel meant the right to hire counsel at one's own expense.

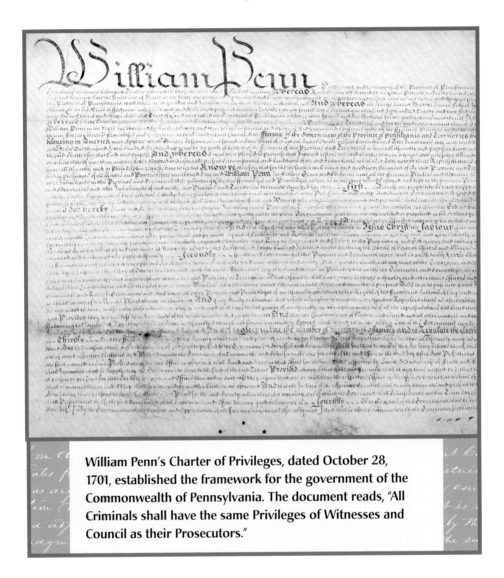

William Penn's Charter of Privileges, dated October 28, 1701, established the framework for the government of the Commonwealth of Pennsylvania. The document reads, "All Criminals shall have the same Privileges of Witnesses and Council as their Prosecutors."

Delaware, Pennsylvania, and Virginia allowed courts to appoint counsel in capital cases when a defendant requested it. New Jersey and Connecticut provided counsel to those who could not afford it in *all* cases, including misdemeanors. Historians and legal scholars, however, are not certain how early state courts applied right-to-counsel laws. Even though the right to counsel was guaranteed either by a state constitution or a state statute, it appears that few defendants hired a lawyer. Many defendants could not afford a lawyer, and many locales of the young nation still had few or no local lawyers.

The Articles of Confederation had intentionally created a weak national government. This weakness, however, eventually led to major disputes between the states. In 1787, delegates from the 13 states met in Philadelphia, Pennsylvania, to improve the Articles of Confederation. The delegates took it a step further. They proposed that the nation's central government be completely reorganized. They drafted the U.S. Constitution, which established a republican form of government with three branches: legislative, judicial, and executive. The legislative branch (Congress) would enact laws. The judicial branch (the courts) would interpret and apply the laws. The executive branch (the president and other departments of the federal government) would enforce the laws. When it went into effect in 1789, the Constitution provided the basic law of the United States.

Two years after the Constitution was ratified, or formally established, 10 amendments—known as the Bill of Rights— were added to guarantee individual liberties. The colonists' conflicts with British authority had broadened the overall concept of liberty in America. These 10 amendments reflected the new nation's commitment to civil rights and justice. The Bill of Rights applied only to the federal government, however. Many states adopted similar provisions in their own constitutions. The rights granted to citizens and the judicial interpretations of these rights, however, varied greatly among the states.

When the delegates were considering constitutional amendments, only two states, Virginia and North Carolina, recommended adding a provision guaranteeing the right to counsel. James Madison of Virginia drafted the language for the proposed amendment. The delegates did not debate Madison's provision. Legal scholars believe that the delegates didn't look closely at Madison's draft because federal courts were unlikely to hear many criminal cases. It remained unaltered and became part of the Bill of Rights as the Sixth Amendment. In full, the Sixth Amendment reads:

> In all criminal prosecutions, the accused shall enjoy the right to a speedy and public trial, by an impartial jury of the State and district wherein the crime shall have been committed, which district shall have been previously ascertained by law, and to be informed of the nature and cause of the accusation; to be confronted with the witnesses against him; to have compulsory process for obtaining witnesses in his favor, and to have the Assistance of Counsel for his defense.[16]

THE BILL OF RIGHTS

The U.S. Constitution spelled out the powers of federal government; its seven articles, however, did not place any restrictions on the government. Several states objected that the proposed Constitution failed to prevent the federal government from infringing on, or violating, individual liberties. These states threatened not to ratify the Constitution unless it guaranteed basic civil rights. Virginia's Thomas Jefferson argued, "A bill of rights is what the people are entitled to against every government on earth, general or particular, and what no just government should refuse, or rest on inference."* To guarantee that the Constitution would be ratified, the delegates at the Constitutional Convention agreed that a bill of rights would be added to the document. Ratified on December 15, 1791, the Bill of Rights consists of the first 10 amendments to the Constitution. These amendments guarantee the basic civil rights of all U.S. citizens, including freedom of speech, freedom of religion, and the right to counsel.

---

* 1787 letter to James Madison; available at "The Bill of Rights." Thomas Jefferson on Politics & Government. http://etext.virginia.edu/jefferson/quotations/jeff0950.htm.

The Sixth Amendment provides many safeguards that protect the rights of those accused of crimes. A defendant must receive fair notice of the criminal charges against him or her. Excessive bail cannot be used to keep a defendant in custody. A defendant has the right to be represented by an attorney. A defendant is entitled to a speedy trial. Criminal trials must be public and tried by an impartial jury. Defendants have the right to face and cross-examine prosecution witnesses. Evidence gathered illegally—either by an unreasonable search of a defendant or his or her property, or by an unreasonable seizure of his or her papers or property—cannot be used against a defendant. A person cannot be tried twice for the same offense (known as double jeopardy). Finally, punishment of those found guilty cannot be excessive or cruel.

THE RIGHT TO COUNSEL IN FEDERAL COURTS

The Sixth Amendment created the right to counsel in federal courts, but the precise nature of that right was not clear. Because there had been no debate on the language of the Sixth Amendment at the Constitutional Convention, the intent of its framers was unknown. The very first Congress passed two laws that perhaps provided some indication of the intended scope of the Sixth Amendment's "right to counsel" clause. Section 35 of the Judiciary Act of 1789 allowed parties in federal courts to handle their own cases personally or with the assistance of counsel. Under the Act of April 30, 1790, a person indicted for treason or any other capital offense was "allowed to make his full defence by counsel learned in the law; and the court before which he is tried, or some judge thereof, shall immediately, upon his request, assign to him such counsel not exceeding two, as he may desire, and they shall have free access to him at all reasonable hours."[17]

The Sixth Amendment guaranteed criminal defendants in federal trials the right to be represented by an attorney. Although the amendment did not establish a right for poor de-

The rights Clarence Earl Gideon fought for were actually guaranteed as far back as the Bill of Rights. The Sixth Amendment promises, "the accused shall enjoy the right to a speedy and public trial . . . and to have the Assistance of Counsel for his defense."

fendants to have counsel supplied free of charge, federal courts soon began appointing counsel for poor defendants in most felony cases. There was no constitutional right or law supporting this practice. No official system was developed to pay attorneys, so the appointment of counsel in federal courts was usually not automatic. The defendant either had to request a lawyer or an attorney had to volunteer to take on the case.

Because the vast majority of criminal cases involved state law, early federal courts tried few criminal cases. Thus, over many decades the Supreme Court only heard a few cases involving the Sixth Amendment. The Court did not hear its first major case involving the Sixth Amendment's right-to-counsel clause until 1938. In *Johnson v. Zerbst,* the petitioner had been convicted of spending several counterfeit $20 bills in South Carolina. Johnson had no attorney at his federal court trial, and he sought a writ of habeas corpus after his conviction. (Zerbst was the warden of the federal prison in which Johnson was jailed.) The Court held that the Sixth Amendment requires appointment of counsel for federal criminal defendants who cannot afford to retain a lawyer. Writing for the Court, Justice Hugo Black asserted that the right to the assistance of counsel "is necessary to insure fundamental human rights of life and liberty."[18] The Court's opinion drew no distinctions between a defendant's right to retain counsel and the right to have counsel provided if the defendant could not afford to hire one. Black stressed that counsel was necessary to satisfy the constitutional rights of defendants in federal trials: "The Sixth Amendment withholds from federal courts, in all criminal proceedings, the power and authority to deprive an accused of his life or liberty unless he has or waives the assistance of counsel."[19] Justice Black further noted,

> The Sixth Amendment stands as a constant admonition that if the constitutional safeguards it provides are lost, justice will not "still be done." It embodies a realistic recognition

of the obvious truth that the average defendant does not have the professional legal skill to protect himself when brought before a tribunal with power to take his life or liberty, wherein the prosecution is presented by experienced and learned counsel.[20]

The Court's ruling in *Johnson v. Zerbst* did not create any controversy. It merely gave constitutional status to the general practice of federal courts. It made clear to all federal judges that defendants in their court had the right to retain counsel and the right to have the court appoint them counsel if they could not afford to hire a lawyer. The *Johnson* decision also avoided uproar because it did not apply to criminal trials in state courts.

THE RIGHT TO COUNSEL IN STATE COURTS

The idea that a person charged with a crime should have a fair trial is one of the most basic principles of the U.S. legal system. The Sixth Amendment guarantees citizens accused "in all criminal prosecutions" the "right to assistance of counsel" for their defense. The Sixth Amendment clearly allowed defendants in federal courts to retain legal counsel. After *Johnson v. Zerbst*, federal courts were compelled to appoint legal counsel if a defendant could not afford to hire an attorney.

The Sixth Amendment did not apply to the states, however. States made their own rules regarding the right to counsel in cases involving state criminal laws. As a result, the legal statutes of the right to counsel—and the actual practices in state courts—varied widely among the states. Most states interpreted the right to counsel clauses in their state constitutions or state statutes to mean only that defendants had the right to hire a lawyer to argue their case in court.

Indiana was the first state to recognize that a poor person was entitled to an attorney at public expense. In *Webb v. Baird* (1853), the Indiana Supreme Court recognized a right to an attorney at public expense for an indigent person accused of a crime. The court based its decision on basic societal principles rather than on the Indiana constitutional or any Indiana law. "It is not to be thought of in a civilized community for a moment that any citizen put in jeopardy of life or liberty should be debarred of counsel because he is too poor to employ such aid," the Indiana court wrote. "No court could be expected to respect itself to sit and hear such a trial. The defense of the poor in such cases is a duty which will at once be conceded as essential to the accused, to the court and to the public."[21]

Few other states followed Indiana's example. In most states, poor defendants accused of even the most serious crimes often had no legal counsel at their trials. Local lawyers would sometimes volunteer to represent poor defendants, but that practice was usually limited to unusual cases, such as when the defendant was very young. Private legal aid programs arose in some large cities. For example, the New York Legal Aid Society began providing legal representation to the poor in 1896. Los Angeles started the first publicly funded legal aid organization, now generally known as public defender offices, in 1914. These organizations typically did not have enough staff to defend all poor defendants. Such programs were rare outside of the largest cities, so access to free legal representation was not widespread.

The first major Supreme Court case involving the right to counsel in state courts was *Powell v. Alabama* (1932). In *Powell*, the Supreme Court held that counsel was required in all state capital trials (trials involving the death penalty). Known popularly as the Scottsboro Boys case, *Powell* was an unusual case: After a hasty trial, an Alabama court sentenced eight black youths to death for the rape of two white women. The defendants had no counsel.

The Court based its decision on the Fourteenth Amendment. Since the passage of that amendment in 1868, many rights and liberties contained in the Bill of Rights have been extended to the states. The Fourteenth Amendment was designed primarily to make former slaves citizens of the United States and the states in which they lived. States were not allowed to "deprive any person of life, liberty, or property, without due process of law."[22] Later Supreme Court decisions interpreted the Fourteenth Amendment to mean that states could not deny constitutional rights to any of its citizens. In its decision, the Court ruled that the due process clause of the Fourteenth Amendment requires that a trial court observe certain fundamental rights. Writing for the Court, Justice George Sutherland asserted, "the right to the aid of counsel is of this fundamental character."[23]

Sutherland made a powerful case for the necessity of counsel at trial:

> The right to be heard would be, in many cases, of little avail if it did not comprehend the right to be heard by counsel. Even the intelligent and educated layman has small and sometimes no skill in the science of law. If charged with crimes, he is incapable, generally, of determining for himself whether the indictment is good or bad. He is unfamiliar with the rules of evidence. Left without the aid of counsel he may be put on trial without a proper charge, and convicted upon incompetent evidence, or evidence irrelevant to the issue or otherwise inadmissible. He lacks both the skill and knowledge adequately to prepare his defense, even though he had a perfect one. He requires the guiding hand of counsel at every step in the proceedings against him. Without it, though he be not guilty, he faces the danger of conviction because he does not know how to establish his innocence.[24]

The Alabama court's failure to give the defendants an opportunity to retain counsel violated due process. The Court acknowledged that, as indigents, the youths could not have retained counsel. Given these unusual circumstances, the Court concluded that "the necessity of counsel was so vital and imperative that the failure of the trial court to make an effective appointment of counsel was likewise a denial of due process within the meaning of the Fourteenth Amendment."[25] The Court pointed to the unusual set of circumstances in the case: the age and inexperience of the defendants, public hostility toward the defendants, distant friends and family, and the possibility of a death sentence. The *Powell* decision did not establish a broad right to counsel. The Court carefully

 THE SCOTTSBORO BOYS

The case of a group of black teenagers charged with raping two white women attracted national attention for more than a decade. On a freight train passing through Alabama in 1931, a group of black teens got into a fight with a group of white teens. A large number of young, homeless, unemployed people had hopped onto the train in Georgia and Tennessee, hoping to find jobs in towns farther west. When the train pulled to a stop near Scottsboro, Alabama, local police broke up the fight. Two young women emerged from a freight car and claimed to have been raped. The police arrested nine black teenagers. Their ages ranged from 12 to 20. In a series of trials, the young men were found guilty. Eight were sentenced to death. The youngest defendant was sentenced to life in prison.

In 1936, the U.S. Supreme Court overturned all of their convictions on the grounds that the defendants' right to counsel had been violated by the set of circumstances surrounding the case. (The Court would overturn later convictions because no blacks had served on the grand juries or on the trial juries.) During the second round of trials, one of the accusers denied being raped. In 1937, charges were dropped against five of the defendants. Three of the defendants were eventually found guilty. The state agreed to consider parole for them, and by 1944 all three were out of jail.

The Scottsboro Boys, as they were dubbed, were unjustly accused of raping two white women in the 1930s. The youths were not allowed counsel and were sentenced to death.

kept its ruling narrow: "In a capital case, where the defendant is unable to employ counsel, and is incapable adequately of making his own defense because of ignorance, feeble mindedness, illiteracy, or the like, it is the duty of the court, whether requested or not, to assign counsel for him as a necessary requisite of due process of law."[26]

Powell made it clear that the assistance of counsel could be a fundamental ingredient for a fair trial in a state trial involving the death penalty. After *Powell*, to avoid the possibility of overturned convictions, all state courts began appointing counsel in capital cases. In noncapital cases, state courts continued to follow their existing practices. In many states, this meant that courts would not appoint counsel for poor defendants.

Ten years after *Powell*, the Supreme Court addressed the issue of whether the right to court-appointed counsel should be extended to noncapital trials in state courts. In *Betts v. Brady* (1942), the Supreme Court held that the Sixth Amendment guarantees counsel in noncapital trials only in federal courts. Smith Betts, a Maryland farmworker, was accused of robbery. At his trial, he had requested a lawyer to represent him. The trial judge denied his request, noting that it was not the practice in that county to appoint counsel for poor defendants. The only exceptions were in cases involving murder or rape (both capital cases). Betts was convicted and sentenced to eight years in prison.

The Supreme Court affirmed Betts's conviction. Writing for the Court, Justice Owen Roberts asserted that the requirements of the due process clause of the Fourteenth Amendment were "less rigid and more fluid"[27] than the guarantees in the Sixth Amendment. He argued that the issue raised by *Betts* was "whether the constraint laid by the [Sixth] Amendment upon the national courts expresses a rule so fundamental and essential to a fair trial, and so, to due process of law, that it is made obligatory upon the States by the Fourteenth Amendment."[28] By a six to three vote, the Court concluded that it was. Examining the common law rules, the practice of English courts, and the constitutions, laws, and practices of the states, Roberts wrote that it was the "considered judgment of the people, their representatives and their courts that appointment of counsel is not a fundamental right essential to a fair trial."[29] Roberts drew a distinction between *Powell v. Alabama* and *Betts*. He asserted,

> while the want of counsel in a particular case may result in a conviction lacking in such fundamental fairness, we cannot say that the [Fourteenth] Amendment embodies an inexorable command that no trial for any offense, or in any court,

can be fairly conducted and justice accorded a defendant who is not represented by counsel.[30]

In his dissenting opinion, Justice Hugo Black disagreed with the majority's decision. He felt that the majority was being overly protective of state interests. He argued that the Fourteenth Amendment made the Sixth Amendment applicable to the states and required the appointment of counsel. He wrote:

> Denial to the poor of the request for counsel in proceedings based on charges of serious crime has long been regarded as shocking to the "universal sense of justice" throughout this country. . . . Most . . . states have shown their agreement by constitutional provisions, statutes, or established practice judicially approved which assure that no man shall be deprived of counsel merely because of his poverty. Any other practice seems to me to defeat the promise of our democratic society to provide equal justice under the law.[31]

Betts affirmed that state legislatures could determine whether to provide free legal assistance to criminal defendants. The Fourteenth Amendment required state courts to ensure that defendants received a fair trial. In noncapital cases, however, the failure to appoint counsel to indigent (poor) defendants would not violate the due process clause unless there were special circumstances. Whether a defendant requesting court-appointed counsel had established the necessary special circumstances would be decided on a case-by-case basis.

In cases following *Betts*, the Supreme Court developed three general categories of special circumstances that required court-appointed counsel. These factors could overlap in some cases:

1. The personal characteristics of the defendant made it unlikely that he or she could present an adequate defense on his or her own.

2. The criminal charges or the defenses to the charges were particularly complicated.

3. The circumstances surrounding the trial raised the possibility of racial prejudice.

Many legal scholars, civil rights organizations, and defense lawyers criticized the *Betts* decision. Two young lawyers, Benjamin Cohen and Erwin Griswold (who would later become dean of Harvard Law School), wrote a letter to the *New York Times*. They asserted, "Most Americans—lawyers and laymen alike—before the decision in *Betts v. Brady* would have thought that the right of the accused to counsel in serious criminal cases was unquestionably a part of our own Bill of Rights."[32]

State courts also encountered problems with the *Betts* decision. Its special circumstances rule did not supply clear guidelines to courts. Some state courts began following the practice of federal courts, appointing counsel when requested by a defendant in a felony case. Other states continued to deny counsel except in capital cases. Because of the misapplication of the *Betts* rule, the number of convictions overturned by the Supreme Court increased over the years. When the Court accepted Clarence Earl Gideon's appeal, the practices of trial courts varied from state to state.

3

The Lawyers
Prepare
Their Briefs

Once the Supreme Court agreed to review *Gideon v. Cochran*, the lawyers for Gideon and the State of Florida began preparing their cases. The attorneys reviewed the circumstances of Gideon's trial. They researched past Supreme Court cases dealing with the right to counsel. Piece by piece, they built their arguments to convince the Court to rule in their favor.

FORTAS PLANS HIS CASE

Abe Fortas knew that he only needed to convince five of the nine justices that the Supreme Court should extend the right to counsel to state criminal trials. He realized that he was asking the Court to overturn *Betts v. Brady*, a case that was only 20 years old. He believed that he needed to achieve more than a narrow victory. Fortas later recalled:

> In this case—a constitutional case of fundamental impor-
> tance, and with political overtones in terms of federal–state
> relations—it seemed to me the responsibility was not just to
> try to win the case but to get as many justices as possible to
> go along with what I considered the right result.[33]

Fortas assumed that he could count on the votes of Chief Justice Earl Warren and justices Hugo Black, William Douglas, and William Brennan. These four justices had publicly expressed their dissatisfaction with the *Betts* decision. Justice Potter Stewart also seemed like a good bet to vote in Gideon's favor. During his four years on the Court, Stewart had voted to overturn the conviction in every case in which the defendant had claimed that he should have a lawyer at his state court trial. Fortas was less certain about how Justice Tom Clark would vote. On the one hand, he had voted against overturning convictions in earlier right-to-counsel cases. Clark, however, had written the Court's opinion in a recent case that outlawed the use of illegally ac-quired evidence in state criminal trials. Fortas guessed that two justices—Felix Frankfurter and John Harlan—were unlikely to vote to overrule *Betts*. Both justices had long been outspoken about their concerns about balancing federal and state powers. They had almost always voted against imposing federal restric-tions on state criminal procedures. The newest justice, Byron White, had only been on the bench for two months. He had the reputation, however, of opposing the expansion of the rights of the accused.

Fortas soon realized that in order to build a strong case, he needed to show the Court the real-life effect of the *Betts* rule. He firmly believed that defendants could get a fair criminal tri-al only if lawyers represented them. Fortas wanted to give the justices a genuine feel for the atmosphere of state criminal courts when a defendant had to represent himself. "What I'd like to have said," he later remarked, "was, 'Let's not talk. Let's go down and watch one of these fellows try to defend himself.'"[34]

Researching the Case

Fortas asked one of his firm's younger partners, Abe Krash, to research the Fourteenth Amendment and the right to counsel. A small team of lawyers at Arnold, Fortas & Porter began analyzing the issues that Gideon's case raised. John Hart Ely, a summer associate who was a student at Yale Law School, worked on the case for two months. He wrote a series of legal memos to Krash and Fortas. These memos covered a wide variety of issues related to the case. One memo, for example, detailed the history of the Court's interpretation of the Fourteenth Amendment.

Ely's most important memo covered how the *Betts* rule was actually applied in the state courts, especially the Florida courts. Ely pored over law review articles that examined the right to counsel in state courts. (Law reviews are publications that contain in-depth articles written by law professors, judges, lawyers, and law students on various legal topics.) Most of the law articles criticized *Betts*. They pointed out its weaknesses and the problems caused by the *Betts* special circumstances rule. Ely concluded that state courts almost always rejected a defendant's claim to the right to counsel. Although the state courts usually used the same language as the Supreme Court and also mentioned the same factors, they rarely came to the same conclusions. "The fact that the United States Supreme Court has reversed the Florida Supreme Court in four right-to-counsel cases since 1959," Ely wrote, "suggests that the two courts have different ideas as to how the factors should be balanced."[35] Ely identified the source of the problem. He noted that in its right-to-counsel decisions over the past 20 years, the Supreme Court had offered more than 20 different factors that state courts should consider. These factors included the complexity of the criminal statute,

Attorney Abe Fortas (pictured here in 1963) had a strong interest in the rights of the accused and agreed to represent Clarence Earl Gideon. Fortas became an associate justice of the U.S. Supreme Court a few years after the *Gideon* hearings.

the defendant's age and education, and the defendant's mental capacity and race. Two other key factors were the defendant's prior experience with the law and the adequacy of the judge's guidance at trial.

In another memo, Ely considered a line of attack that Fortas had proposed. Fortas wanted to argue that *Betts* actually harmed the federal–state relationship that the Court had sought to protect. In *Betts*, the Court had formulated the special circumstances approach in order to minimize federal interference in the states' control of their own courts. Fortas felt that by requiring the appointment of counsel in state court cases, the Court would cause less intrusion on state criminal processes. A clear-cut rule on the appointment of counsel would lead to less confusion on the part of state court judges. A clear-cut rule would also result in fewer appeals to the Supreme Court. The *Betts* rule required state courts to guess how to apply the Supreme Court's standards. If the state court made a wrong decision in refusing to appoint legal counsel for the defendant, the state would have to try the case over again. The *Betts* rule placed the trial judge in a tough spot. The judge often could not foresee how a trial would play out. Even a case that seemed simple at the outset could turn out to be difficult. Even an educated defendant could struggle to defend himself. By providing states with the discretion to deny defendants counsel, the *Betts* rule set up a system in which the Supreme Court was constantly reviewing the decisions of state courts.

In other memos, Ely pointed out additional problems with the special circumstances rule. Errors by the trial judge were unlikely to be corrected on appeal. Unlike Gideon, few convicts had the knowledge, ability, and ambition to file appeals successfully. Ely also questioned the logic of the distinction the Court had drawn between requiring counsel in capital cases (where the death sentence is possible) but not in noncapital cases. He noted that many noncapital cases are equally or more complicated than capital cases. Ely cautioned that it would be a mistake to argue that the Fourteenth Amendment had made the Sixth Amendment applicable to the states. The Court had flatly rejected this argument in earlier cases. Instead, he suggested that Fortas should argue that the right to counsel was fundamental.

Therefore, the right to counsel was implicit in the Fourteenth Amendment's guarantee of due process of law.

Ely also thought that an argument involving the Fourteenth Amendment's equal protection clause would bolster Gideon's case. He pointed out a sentence from Justice Black's opinion in *Griffin v. Illinois* (1956). In that case, the Court held that a state denied the defendant equal protection of the law. The state required payment for trial records in order to appeal, thus preventing poor convicts from appealing their cases. Black wrote: "There can be no equal justice where the kind of trial a man gets depends on the amount of money he had."[36]

Ely then looked closely at the transcript of Gideon's trial. He detailed the many possible errors that the trial judge made. He also noted examples of unfairness toward Gideon. Ely argued,

> Here is a trial in which the defendant was skillful and the judge made every effort to protect his rights. Yet even here close examination of the law and of the facts reveals that defendant was repeatedly hurt by lack of counsel. If such prejudice occurred in this trial, it would seem that there is *no* trial in which counsel is unnecessary.[37]

Fortas later remarked,

> I am convinced that this judge in Panama City, Florida, tried to help Gideon defend himself. He just did a bad job, as any judge would; it's not a judge's role to be a defense counsel. He made mistakes. But how corrosive it is for federal–state relations to have a federal court tell that judge later that he did not do an adequate job?[38]

Preparing the Briefs

Briefs for *Gideon v. Cochran* were due in early November 1962. In late summer, John Hart Ely returned to Yale for his final year of law school. Two junior lawyers at Arnold, Fortas & Porter took over for him. In writing the first draft of Gideon's brief, Ralph Temple and Bruce Montgomery covered the constitutional and legal issues involved in the case. They also dealt with the practical issues. They discussed how far the right to counsel should extend: Should states provide counsel at the trial stage, at the arrest stage, or at questionings and lineups before an arrest? The two attorneys also examined the effect of overruling *Betts* on the status of prisoners throughout the country. One concern underlying Gideon's appeal was what overturning his conviction would mean to every prisoner who had been convicted without the benefit of legal counsel. Would the *Gideon* decision be narrow, only applying to future trials? Or would these prisoners be granted new trials or released outright?

Temple and Montgomery felt that overturning Gideon's conviction would not create a widespread problem. They discovered that many states already appointed counsel for the poor in their criminal courts. University of Minnesota law professor Yale Kamisar had researched this very issue. The *University of Chicago Law Review* would soon publish an article that he had written on the topic. The article examined how the states provided attorneys for poor defendants. Kamisar heard about Gideon's case and sent Fortas a copy of his article. It showed that when *Betts* was decided in 1942, 30 states provided legal counsel to the poor as a matter of right in felony cases. Twenty years later, as the Court was set to hear Gideon's appeal, 37 states provided legal counsel to the poor in felony cases. Kamisar noted that 13 states did not require the appointment of legal counsel except in capital cases. In 8 of these states, trial judges sometimes appointed counsel, even though there was no statute or formal court rule. Only five states did not assure counsel for poor defendants, except in capital cases. Those states were Alabama, Florida, Mississippi, North Carolina, and South Carolina. Kamisar's research

Enacted to extend liberties to slaves in the United States, the Fourteenth Amendment was cited by Gideon in his petition as guaranteeing that no state shall take any citizen's "life, liberty, or property without due process of law."

showed that in many larger cities in these 13 states, poor defendants charged with felonies were likely to be given lawyers. There were no guarantees, however. In Gideon's home state of Florida, for example, three large cities—Miami, Tampa, and Fort Lauderdale—had local public defenders. In smaller cities and rural areas, courts were unlikely to appoint counsel for poor defendants. Kamisar also showed that 24 states provided counsel for defendants charged with misdemeanors.

The Brief for Gideon

Fortas reviewed the draft brief. He added comments, and Abe Krash wrote the final version of the brief. During the month he worked on the brief, Krash spent six hours a day on it. Fortas's office filed the brief for Gideon on November 21, 1962. It was 53 pages long. In the brief, Fortas did not try to establish any special circumstances for Gideon. He did not argue that the Fourteenth Amendment should incorporate the Sixth Amendment. He asserted that *Betts* should be overturned.

In the brief's introduction, Fortas laid out the basics of his case. He argued that the administration of the *Betts* rule since 1942 "had not been a happy one. . . . The quality of criminal justice and the relations between the federal and state courts have suffered."[39] The brief pointed out that limiting the appointment of counsel to only those cases where there could be special needs had not resulted in fundamental fairness in many cases. Furthermore, the case-by-case determination of special circumstances resulted in a "corrosive and irritating process of case-by-case review"[40] by federal courts.

Fortas directed the court's attention to a separate section at the end of the brief. The section detailed how a lawyer would have protected Gideon's rights in his trial. It showed "that he did not have a fair trial in the constitutional sense. But it is our opinion that these points [of analysis] are not peculiar to Gideon's case. We believe . . . [they] are present in every criminal prosecution."[41]

The body of the brief was organized into five sections. The first section dealt with the issue of whether the Fourteenth Amendment requires that counsel be appointed to represent an indigent defendant in every criminal case involving a serious offense. In this section, Fortas argued that various legal doctrines supported his case. He asserted, "The aid of counsel is indispensable to a fair hearing."[42] He noted the requirement of appointed counsel in federal criminal trials. He stressed that the trial judge could not be relied on to protect the defendant's right because a judge is supposed to be neutral. Fortas went even further, arguing that the distinction between capital and noncapital cases was wrong. The due process clause protects not only a citizen's "life" but also "liberty" and "property."[43] Finally, he claimed that, as shown by the Court's ruling in *Griffin v. Illinois*, the equal protection clause requires provision of counsel.

The brief's second section evaluated the argument that the demands of federalism supported maintaining the *Betts* ruling. Here, Fortas used the Kamisar article to show that a strong majority of states currently appointed counsel in all felony cases as a matter of law or practice. This key argument undercut the majority opinion in *Betts*. The Court had held that the states did not regard counsel as a "fundamental right, essential to a fair trial."[44] Fortas argued that *Betts* did not smooth out the relationship between the states and the federal courts. Instead, the brief noted, "*Betts v. Brady* has created friction between the states and the federal courts" because "it does not prescribe a clear-cut standard which the state courts can follow."[45] In other words, the special circumstances rule had lead to federal courts constantly overruling state court decisions. Since *Betts*, prisoners had flooded the Court with habeas corpus petitions claiming that they had been wrongly denied appointed counsel at their trials. Fortas argued that overruling *Betts* would still provide flexibility for the states. They could experiment with different systems for providing counsel. These systems could be public defender offices, private voluntary associations, or court-appointed counsel.

The third section of the brief pointed out that the *Betts* ruling had not provided an acceptable standard for judicial administration. The Supreme Court's own decisions using the special circumstances approach had been confusing and inconsistent. In practice, state courts rarely found reason to appoint counsel. This occurred even when the circumstances, on later review, seemed to show that counsel should have been provided.

The brief's fourth section discussed the issue of when counsel should be appointed. Fortas argued that counsel should be provided at least at the trial stage. He suggested that an accused should have the right to consult a lawyer after he or she was arrested. He admitted that Gideon's case involved only the right to counsel at the trial stage.

In the fifth and final section of the brief, Fortas dealt with the issue of the practical impact if the Court overruled *Betts*. What would happen to all those prisoners who didn't have a lawyer at their trial? Fortas noted that anyone whose conviction would be reversed as a result of *Gideon* would be subject to retrial. Fortas ended the brief by quoting a letter that had appeared years earlier in the *New York Times*. Two lawyers, Erwin Griswold and Benjamin Cohen, had written to the editors of the newspaper when the *Betts* decision had been announced in 1942. They wrote,

> At a critical period in world history *Betts v. Brady* tilts the scales against the safeguarding of one of the most precious rights of man. For in a free world no man should be condemned to penal servitude for years without having the right to counsel to defend him. The right of counsel, for the poor as well as the rich, is an indispensable safeguard of freedom and justice under law.[46]

As required by Court rules, Fortas mailed the brief to the opposing counsel, the attorney general of Florida. He also sent a copy to his client. Gideon wrote back:

Dear Sir:

This is to thank you for sending me a copy of the brief you have prepared and presented to the Supreme Court for my cause. Ever[y]one and myself thinks it is a very wonderful and brilliant document.

I do not know how you have enticed the general public to take such an interest in this cause. But I must say it makes me feel very good.[47]

FLORIDA PREPARES ITS BRIEF

Florida attorney general Richard W. Erwin assigned the *Gideon* case to a young lawyer in his office's criminal division. Assistant Attorney General Bruce Robert Jacob was only 26 years old when Gideon's appeal was granted. He had only two years of experience. Erwin entrusted him with the task of preparing the case for the State of Florida. Jacob was familiar with the case because he had drafted Erwin's letter in response to Gideon's petitions to the Supreme Court.

Jacob realized that he faced an uphill battle. Like Fortas, he knew that four of the justices were likely to vote against him. His job, however, was to present his side's best argument. His 74-page brief argued that *Betts v. Brady* was still good law. It concluded that Gideon was not entitled to counsel under existing rule established by *Betts*. Jacob reviewed the cases that followed *Betts*. He then argued that Gideon had "made no affirmative showing of any circumstances of unfairness which would have entitled him to counsel under the Fourteenth Amendment." These circumstances included "age, experience, mental capacity, familiarity or unfamiliarity with court procedure, or the complexity of the legal issues presented by the charge."[48] The transcript of trial proved that he had a fair trial. Jacob wrote, "He took an active role in his defense and showed that he possessed much skill and facility in questioning witnesses."[49] He pointed out that Gideon's arrest record showed that he had some familiarity with courts and criminal procedure.

The main part of the brief provided many reasons why *Betts* should not be overturned. The brief argued that there was no historical basis "for requiring states to automatically appoint counsel in all cases."[50] Jacob asserted that the Sixth Amendment was only intended to do away with the old English common law rule that banned counsel for defendants in felony cases.

Next, Jacob argued that the federal system of the United States did not impose a uniform system of criminal procedures. The Constitution gave the states much leeway in determining their own practices in state court trials. He argued that if the Court adopted "an inflexible rule requiring automatic appointment in every case," it would "defeat the very desirable possibility of state experiment in the field of criminal procedure."[51] Jacob asserted that the *Betts* rule provided a clear and workable standard for state judges to use in deciding whether they should appoint counsel. He argued that the inconsistencies noted in the Fortas brief were the normal outcomes under the common law. Jacob summed up this section: "The *Betts* approach is the common law approach, consisting of the development of a body of law on a case-by-case basis, and lawyers for centuries have thrived in distinguishing one case from another on the basis of factual situations and circumstances."[52]

Jacob then considered the other issues that Gideon's case presented. Jacob agreed that many states required the appointment of counsel. He pointed out that the rules of the states varied greatly. Because there was not agreement among the states, Fortas had overstated the current state of the law. He could not claim that the right to appointed counsel was fundamental. Jacob also noted that incorporation of the Sixth Amendment by the Fourteenth Amendment would have grave consequences. He asserted that it would be impossible to draw the line at felonies. Courts would be compelled to appoint counsel in misdemeanor trials as well. This would strain the legal system. There would be more trials. Lawyers would be overwhelmed. The growing expenses would be passed on to taxpayers.

Jacob also argued that the equal protection clause of Fourteenth Amendment does not require appointment of counsel to the poor. If it did, then states would have to provide all sorts of things for poor defendants. They would have to provide counsel for appeals, pay for bail, and so forth.

Jacob then turned to the practical consequences of overturning *Betts*. He pointed out that, in Florida, 5,093 of the 7,836 prisoners in custody had not been represented by an attorney at trial. Jacob provided a stark look into the future: "If *Betts* should be overruled by this Court in this instant case, as many as 5,093 hardened criminals may be eligible to be released in one mass exodus in Florida alone, not to mention other states."[53] Jacob ended his brief with a simple request: "If this Court should decide to overrule *Betts*, respondent respectfully requests that it be accomplished in such way as to prevent the new rule from operating retrospectively."[54] He was asking that if the Court decided to expand the right to counsel, then its new standard should not apply to convicts already in jail. This would include Clarence Earl Gideon.

Jacob had one additional item to support his position. He had received a letter from Robert L. McCrary, Jr., the judge who presided over Gideon's trial. McCrary wrote that, in his opinion, "Gideon had both the mental capacity and the experience in the courtroom at previous trials to adequately conduct his defense. . . . In my opinion, he did as well as most lawyers could have done in handling his case."[55] Jacob did not include the letter in brief. Instead, he sent it to the Court clerk, who placed it in the Gideon file. The justices would consider it along with the briefs and all the other documents in the case.

"FRIEND OF THE COURT" BRIEFS

Jacob drafted a letter to the attorneys general in the 49 other states. He hoped to find support among the other states for his argument that *Betts* should not be overruled. It was not unusual for states to support other states in opposing federal restraints on state laws or procedures. The letter was sent out under Attorney General Erwin's signature. It read:

> Four members of the present Court have expressed the view, at one time or another, that *Betts* should be overruled and that the concept of the right to counsel under the Sixth Amendment should be embraced within the due-process clause of the Fourteenth Amendment. If the minority can obtain one more vote, *Betts* will be overruled and the States will, in effect, be mandatorily required to appoint counsel in all felony cases. Such a decision would infringe on the rights of the states to determine their own rules of criminal procedure.[56]

The letter went on to ask the attorneys general to provide any advice or information that would help his office prepare its brief for the *Gideon* case. In addition, Erwin invited each of the attorneys general to file an *amicus curaie* (from the Latin phrase for "a friend of the court") brief in support of *Betts*. The Supreme Court sometimes allows a person or organization that is not a party to a case to submit an amicus curaie brief to advise the Court on a legal issue involved in the case.

Much to Jacob's surprise, the first responses to Erwin's letter were either lukewarm or noncommittal. Then he received a shocker. Minnesota's attorney general, Walter Mondale, wrote:

> I believe in federalism and states' rights too. But I also believe in the Bill of Rights. . . . Nobody knows better than an attorney general or a prosecuting attorney that in this day and age furnishing an attorney to those felony defendants who can't afford to hire one is "fair and feasible." . . . Nobody knows better than we do that rules of criminal law and procedure which baffle trained professionals can only overwhelm the uninitiated. . . . Since I believe that any person charged with a felony should be accorded a right to be represented by counsel regardless of his financial condition,

I would welcome the courts' imposition of a requirement of appointment to counsel in all state felony prosecutions.[57]

Mondale recognized that it was Jacob's job to support his state's law. However, he sent copies of the letters to the attorney general of Massachusetts, Edward McCormack, Jr. McCormack passed the letters along to Gerald Berlin, the head of his office's civil rights division. Berlin decided to write an amicus curiae brief on behalf of Gideon. He received help from several Harvard Law School faculty members and students. Mondale and McCormack persuaded the attorneys general of 23 other states to cosign the brief. Three of the states—Hawaii, Maine, and Rhode Island—did not even require trial judges to appoint counsel in felony cases. The attorneys' general brief concluded:

THE AMICUS CURIAE BRIEF

The Rules of the Supreme Court describes the "friend of the court" brief: "An *amicus curiae* brief that brings to the attention of the Court relevant matter not already brought to its attention by the parties may be of considerable help to the Court."* Under federal rules of procedure, an amicus curiae brief can be filed in two ways. All parties must agree that the brief can be filed, or the court must request that the brief be filed. If one of the parties does not consent to the filing of an amicus curiae brief, the filer can ask the Court for permission to submit it. Because it is assumed that they have an interest in all cases, the United States government and the states are always allowed to file an amicus curiae brief.

* "Rule 37." Rules of the Supreme Court of the United States. http://www.supremecourtus.gov/ctrules/rulesofthecourt.pdf.

Walter Mondale (pictured above in 1960) sent out an important letter in favor of defendants' rights to counsel. "I would welcome the courts' imposition of a requirement of appointment to counsel in all state felony prosecutions," the Minnesota attorney general wrote.

Betts v. Brady . . . has spawned 20 years of bad law. That in the world of today a man may be condemned to penal servitude for lack of means to supply counsel for his defense is unthinkable. We respectfully urge that the conviction below be reversed and that the Court require that all persons tried for a felony in a state court shall have the right to counsel as a matter of due process of law and of equal protection of the laws.[58]

Oregon decided to file an amicus curiae brief on its own. Its brief described the state's experience under a recent law that allowed prisoners to petition the state court for relief of claimed violations of their federal constitutional rights. The Oregon brief concluded:

> The experience of the State of Oregon tends to indicate that it would provide greater protection of constitutional rights, and would be less expensive, to insist upon counsel in each original criminal proceeding than to attempt by a postconviction proceeding to recover justices lost by defects at the trial.[59]

When he read these briefs, Fortas was encouraged. He was also surprised that so many states would go on record urging the Supreme Court to overrule *Betts*.

Two states—Alabama and North Carolina—jointly filed an amicus curiae brief supporting Florida's position. Written by Alabama assistant attorney general George Mentz, it made a strong appeal for federalism and states' rights. Mentz wrote,

> Even with its exposure to occasional abuses, the rule of *Betts v. Brady* remains the best one for our American way of life. Any decision to make mandatory the appointment of counsel for all indigents charged with crime in state courts should come not for this Court but from the people of the individual states acting through their elected legislatures or judges.[60]

The American Civil Liberties Union (ACLU), a nonprofit organization dedicated to protecting civil liberties, filed an amicus curiae brief supporting Gideon. Its brief focused on how appellate courts in states without a rule for automatic counsel handled right-to-counsel cases. Its research showed that those courts rarely found special circumstances that would require a lawyer. In 138 appeals court decisions, only 11 found that the trial judge had made a mistake in not appointing counsel.

EQUAL·JUSTICE·UNDER·LAW·

4

The Supreme Court's Decision

After preparing and submitting their briefs, the lawyers prepared for the next stage of the *Gideon* case: oral arguments. Fortas and Jacob would each have one hour to make a case before the nine justices of the Supreme Court. For *Gideon*, the Court also took an unusual step. It allowed 30 minutes of argument by a friend of the court on each side. J. Lee Rankin of the American Civil Liberties Union would argue in favor of Gideon. Assistant Attorney General George Mentz of Alabama would argue in favor of Florida. Soon after the oral arguments, the justices would cast their votes to decide Gideon's fate.

THE ORAL ARGUMENTS

On January 15, 1963, lawyers, journalists, and visitors crowded the chamber of the Supreme Court. The Court Crier struck his gavel on a wooden block. Everyone rose from his or her seat. The nine justices of the Supreme Court filed through the red curtain behind their bench. The Crier then announced the traditional phrase that opens each session of the Court: "Oyez, oyez, oyez. All persons having business before the honorable, the Supreme Court of the United States, are admonished to draw near and give their attention, for the Court is now sitting. God save the United States and this honorable Court."[61]

The justices heard the oral arguments for another case that morning. Chief Justice Earl Warren then called Gideon's case. The lawyers for each side moved forward. They took their seats at two long tables situated in front of the justices' bench.

Following Court rules, the party who had appealed the lower court's decision spoke first. Fortas walked over to a lectern located between the two counsel tables. He began his presentation with the customary phrase: "Mr. Chief Justice, may it please the Court. . ."[62] and reviewed the facts of the case. He covered the break-in and Gideon's attempt to represent himself at trial. He then turned to the legal issues that the Court would be weighing. "The record does not indicate that Clarence Earl Gideon was a person of low intelligence or that the judge was unfair to him," Fortas stated. "But to me this case shows the basic difficulty with *Betts versus Brady*. It shows that no man, however intelligent, can conduct his own defense adequately."[63]

Justice Harlan interrupted with a question. Harlan was the Court's strongest supporter of maintaining states' rights. "That's not the point, is it, Mr. Fortas? *Betts* didn't go on the assumption that a man can do as well without an attorney as he can with one, did it? Everyone knows this isn't so."[64] Fortas responded smoothly,

I entirely agree, Mr. Justice Harlan, with the point you are making: Namely, that of course a man cannot have a fair trial without a lawyer, but *Betts* held that this consideration was outweighed by the demands of federalism. . . . I believe this case dramatically illustrates that you cannot have a fair trial without counsel. Under our adversary system of

THE JUSTICES WHO DECIDED GIDEON'S CASE

The Supreme Court justices who heard *Gideon v. Wainwright* came from a variety of backgrounds. Chief Justice Earl Warren had served as attorney general and governor of California. He had been the Republican candidate for vice president in 1948. Hugo Black, a former senator from Alabama, had written a strong dissent in *Betts v. Brady*. Like Black, William O. Douglas, a former law school professional from the state of Washington, had expressed doubts about the *Betts* special circumstances rule. Tom Clark had served as U.S. attorney general in the Truman administration. John Marshall Harlan was a former Wall Street lawyer and the grandson of an earlier Supreme Court justice with the same name. He was known as the Court's strongest advocate for avoiding federal intrusion into state matters.

William Brennan, a former New Jersey Supreme Court justice, was a Democrat who had been appointed to the Court by Republican president Dwight Eisenhower. Another Eisenhower appointee, Potter Stewart had been a respected federal appeals court justice. Byron White, a former college football star and Rhodes scholar, had been a prominent lawyer in Colorado and served as a deputy U.S. attorney general. President John Kennedy had recently appointed Arthur Goldberg as the Court's newest member. An experienced labor lawyer, Goldberg had served as the secretary of labor in the Kennedy administration.

justice, how can our civilized nation pretend that there is a fair trial without the counsel for the prosecution doing all he can within the limits of decency, and the counsel for the defense doing his best within the same limits, and from that clash will emerge the truth?[65]

Fortas then described the difficulties that defendants faced when representing themselves at trial. He asserted,

> I do believe that in some of this Court's decisions there has been a tendency from time to time, because of the pull of federalism . . . to forget the realities of what happens downstairs, of what happens to these poor, miserable, indigent people when they are arrested and they are brought into the jail and they are questioned and later on they are brought in these strange and awesome circumstances before a magistrate, and later on they are brought before a court; and there, Clarence Earl Gideon, defend yourself.[66]

He then offered another example to show how hard it is for defendants to represent themselves. He described the actions of a famous attorney, Clarence Darrow (1857–1938). "I was reminded the other night, as I was pondering this case, of Clarence Darrow when he was prosecuted for trying to fix a jury," Fortas said. "The first thing he realized was that he needed a lawyer—he, one of the country's greatest criminal lawyers."[67]

Fortas then presented his key argument to convince the Court to overturn *Betts*. He suggested that the *Betts* ruling resulted in *more* federal intrusion into the criminal procedures of state courts. He asserted,

> I believe in federalism. . . . But I feel that Betts against Brady does not incorporate a proper regard for federalism. It requires a case-by-case supervision by this Court of state criminal proceedings, and that cannot be wholesome. . . . Intervention should be in the least abrasive, least corrosive way possible.[68]

Fortas described the bumpy road that the right to counsel had traveled from the Supreme Court's ruling in *Powell v. Alabama* to its recent decisions in which the Court applied the *Betts* "special circumstances" rule. He pointed to the research conducted by law professor Yale Kamisar. The professor's research showed that 37 states always provided legal counsel for poor defendants in felony trials. Eight other states often provided counsel in felony trials. Fortas stressed that only five states did not normally provide counsel for poor defendants, except in capital cases. He concluded that the evolving attitude of states toward the right to counsel made overturning *Betts* easier: "I believe we can confidently say that overruling *Betts versus Brady* at this time would be in accord with the opinion of those entitled to an opinion."[69]

In responding to a question by Justice Potter Stewart, Fortas confirmed that he was not arguing in this case that the Fourteenth Amendment should incorporate the Sixth Amendment. He told the Court that he supported the concept of incorporation. He noted, however that "I cannot as an advocate make that argument because this Court has rejected it so many times."[70]

At that point, a red light lit up, indicating that Fortas's time had expired. The Chief Justice gave Fortas five extra minutes to speak after Jacob's presentation. He granted Jacob the same amount of additional time.

Next, J. Lee Rankin, representing the American Civil Liberties Union, stepped up to the lectern. He focused on the larger issues that Gideon's case raised. He argued, "Betts against Brady is built upon the premise that generally you can get a fair trial without counsel. And there's where I think it's unsound."[71]

After a lunch break, Bruce Jacob began his presentation. It was his first appearance before the Court. He appeared nervous. He later remarked, "It was nothing like I expected. It was so informal—I just couldn't believe it."[72] Jacob tried to make his case, but the justices constantly peppered him with questions.

J. Lee Rankin, an attorney representing the American Civil Liberties Union, spoke to the court in favor of Gideon. Nearly a decade earlier, Rankin had argued on behalf of the plaintiffs in the landmark case *Brown v. Board of Education*, which ruled that the "separate but equal" segregation in U.S. public schools was unconstitutional.

In one exchange with the justices, Jacob summarized the State of Florida's position:

> *Justice Black:* Why isn't [*Betts*] as much interference with the states as an absolute rule [requiring appointment of counsel]? One of my reactions to *Betts* was the uncertainty in which it leaves the states.
>
> *Jacob:* I don't think *Betts* is that unclear.
>
> *Justice Black:* How do you know what the "special circumstances" are?
>
> *Jacob:* Each time this Court decides a case, we know another special circumstance.
>
> *Justice Brennan:* In recent years—in four cases I think—we have reversed cases from your state every time.
>
> *Jacob:* We prefer case-by-case adjudication.... It may not be precise, but we prefer it that way because it gives the state some freedom in devising its own rules of criminal procedure.[73]

Jacob then addressed a practical concern: the consequences of overturning *Betts*. He asserted that it would be a "tremendous burden on the taxpayer"[74] for the Court to require states to provide counsel for defendants who could not afford to hire their own attorney. He pointed out that there were 5,093 convicts in Florida prisons who were tried without counsel. They might be eligible for release if the Court overturned *Betts*. "If the Court does reverse, we implore it to find some way not to make it retroactive. We have followed *Betts* in good faith."[75]

George Mentz, representing the State of Alabama, followed Jacob. The experienced lawyer summarized his state's position, stating "I candidly admit that it would be desirable for the states to furnish counsel in all criminal cases. But we say the states should have the right to make that decision themselves."[76]

In his five-minute closing remarks, Fortas pounded home his message:

I think that Betts and Brady was wrong when it was decided. I think time has made that clear. And I think time has now made it possible for the correct rule, the civilized rule, the rule of American constitutionalism, the rule of due process to be stated by this Court with limited disturbances to the states.[77]

THE COURT ANNOUNCES ITS DECISION

The justices usually cast their votes on a case at the Friday conference immediately following the case's oral arguments. These conferences are held in strict confidence, so it is unknown exactly what the justices discussed before voting on the *Gideon* case.

On Monday, March 18, 1963, the Court announced its decision in *Gideon v. Wainwright*. (By this time, Louie Wainwright had replaced H.G. Cochran, Jr., as director of the Florida Division of Corrections.) Justice Hugo Black, who had written a dissenting opinion in *Betts v. Brady* 21 years earlier, read the opinion. Speaking to the assembled audience, Black reviewed the case's path to the Supreme Court. He then stated the Court's ruling in the case: "When we granted certiorari in this case, we asked the lawyers on both sides to argue to us whether we should reconsider the case. We do reconsider *Betts and Brady*, and we reach the opposing conclusion."[78]

Black continued reading the opinion. It became clear that the Court had not based its opinion on using the Fourteenth Amendment to incorporate the Sixth Amendment. Black wrote:

We accept *Betts v. Brady*'s assumption, based as it was on our prior cases, that a provision of the Bill of Rights which is "fundamental and essential to a fair trial" is made obligatory on the states by the Fourteenth Amendment. We think the Court in *Betts* was wrong, however, in concluding that the Sixth Amendment's guarantee of counsel is not one of these fundamental rights.[79]

Black then traced the development of the right to counsel. He pointed out the cases, such as *Powell v. Alabama* and *Johnson v. Zerbst*, that interpreted the Sixth Amendment to require counsel in capital cases and federal criminal trials, respectively. He then noted that *Betts* had made an "abrupt break" from these cases:

> Not only these precedents but also reason and reflection require us to recognize that in our adversary system of

SUPREME COURT OPINIONS

Once the justices have cast their votes on a case, one justice writes the Court's opinion. If the chief justice voted with the majority, he writes the opinion or assigns it to one of the other justices in the majority. If the chief justice did not vote with the majority, the majority's most senior justice either writes the opinion or assigns it to another justice in the majority.

Each justice can write his or her own opinion on any case. A justice can write a concurring opinion that agrees with the majority but bases the justice's decision on a different rationale. A justice can write a dissenting opinion that disagrees with the majority and the reasoning of its decision.

The draft opinions for a case are circulated among the justices for comment. Sometimes a draft opinion will change a justice's vote or thinking about a case. Once all the comments have been returned, a justice will revise the draft and write his or her final opinion. The majority, concurring (if any), and dissenting (if any) opinions of the case are printed together and distributed when the Court's decision is announced.

criminal justice, any person haled into court, who is too poor to hire a lawyer, cannot be assured a fair trial unless counsel is provided for him. This seems to us to be an obvious truth. Governments, both state and federal, quite properly spend vast sums of money to establish machinery to try defendants accused of crime. Lawyers to prosecute are everywhere deemed essential to protect the public's interest in an orderly society. Similarly, there are few defendants charged with crime, few indeed, who fail to hire the best lawyers they can get to prepare and present their defenses. That government hires lawyers to prosecute and defendants who have the money hire lawyers to defend are the strongest indications of the widespread belief that lawyers in criminal courts are necessities, not luxuries. The right of one charged with crime to counsel may not be deemed fundamental and essential to fair trials in some countries, but it is in ours.[80]

The majority opinion concluded:

The Court in *Betts v. Brady* departed from the sound wisdom upon which the Court's holding in *Powell v. Alabama* rested. Florida, supported by two other States, has asked that *Betts v. Brady* be left intact. Twenty-two States, as friends of the Court, argue that *Betts* was "an anachronism when handed down" and that it should now be overruled. We agree.

The judgment is reversed and the cause is remanded to the Supreme Court of Florida for further action not inconsistent with this opinion.[81]

The vote was unanimous, meaning that all nine judges voted to reverse Gideon's conviction. Justices Douglas, Clark, and Harlan wrote concurring opinions. Each agreed that *Betts* should be overturned, but they each based their decisions on different legal theories. Justice Black later confided to a friend, "When *Betts v. Brady* was decided, I never thought I'd live to see it overruled."[82]

THIRTY-FIVE CENTS   OCTOBER 9, 1964

TIME

THE WEEKLY NEWSMAGAZINE

That Activist Supreme Court

JUSTICE
BLACK

VOL. 84 NO. 15

Justice Hugo Black, *Time* magazine's October 9, 1964, cover subject, was one of the U.S. Supreme Court's most influential and longest-serving members. Black read the opinion in the *Gideon* case, announcing that *Betts v. Brady* had been overruled, and overturning the conviction of Clarence Earl Gideon.

The Court had ruled that an indigent person accused of a felony was entitled to the appointment of defense counsel at state expense. The decision, however, left questions unanswered. What type of criminal cases did it cover? Were misdemeanors included? At what stage of legal proceedings is counsel required? Did the decision apply to persons already in prison? Would those convicted without counsel receive new trials or be released outright? The Court seemed to leave these questions for later cases.

THE DESTINY OF CLARENCE EARL GIDEON

The Supreme Court's decision in *Gideon v. Wainwright* did not determine the ultimate legal fate of Clarence Earl Gideon. The Court's ruling only entitled him to a new trial, this time with the assistance of legal counsel.

After the Court's decision, Abe Fortas contacted Tobias Simon, an ACLU lawyer in Miami, Florida. Simon visited Gideon in prison to discuss his upcoming trial. Gideon insisted that a new trial would constitute double jeopardy, or trying a person for the same crime a second time. The Sixth Amendment forbids this. Under U.S. law, however, a new trial won by a prisoner as a result of his own appeal is not double jeopardy because he was not acquitted at the first trial.

Gideon also wanted his trial moved from Panama City because he was convinced that he could not get a fair trial there. His request was denied. Gideon's court date was scheduled for July 5, 1963. His case would be tried before Robert L. McCrary, Jr., the same judge who had presided over Gideon's first trial. On the day of the trial, Irwin Block, an experienced Miami criminal lawyer, joined Simon at the defense table. Gideon had earlier agreed to be represented by Simon. He now refused to be represented by either attorney, apparently because they would not present Gideon's double jeopardy argument to the court. Exasperated, Judge McCrary dismissed Simon and Block. He refused to allow Gideon to represent himself, however. He asked Gideon whether there was a local lawyer who would be acceptable. Gideon said that he wanted W. Fred Turner to represent him. "For the record," McCrary quickly said, "I am going to appoint Mr. Turner to represent this defendant."[83] He set a new trial date.

On August 5, 1963, Gideon's new trial began. He had chosen counsel wisely. Turner knew his way around the community and the Panama City court. During jury selection, Turner asked McCrary to dismiss two potential jurors. He later revealed why he had dropped the two men. He knew that one disapproved of people who, like Gideon, drank alcohol and that the other had the reputation of being a juror who always voted for conviction. Turner later observed that, with potential jurors, "you've got to know who they are, what they think."[84]

The prosecutor again called Henry Cook as his key witness. He told the same story that he gave at Gideon's first trial. Turner began his cross-examination by asking who had dropped him off in front of the pool hall that night. Cook had trouble remembering. Turner suggested a few names—local hoodlums. Turner then asked, "Why did they put you off two blocks from your home when they'd driven you sixty miles [from Apalachicola]?"[85] He then asked Cook why he was hanging out in front of the pool hall, waiting for it to open at 7 A.M. Turner expressed disbelief that Cook would wait outside for hours when he was only two blocks from home. He suggested that perhaps Cook's friends had wanted a drink and had broken into the pool hall to grab some beer and wine. Cook had been their lookout. Turner hinted that this explained why he was standing around outside when the police arrived.

Turner then peppered Cook with questions about the pool hall. In preparing for trial, Turner had investigated the crime scene. He asked Cook whether he had entered the pool hall. Had he taken any beers? How could he see inside, given that advertising signs blocked the front windows? Weren't the windows in the alley too high to see into? Turner then asked Cook, "Ever been convicted of a felony?" Cook replied, "No sir, not convicted. I stole a car and was put on probation."[86] At Gideon's first trial, Cook had stated only that he had not been convicted of a felony. Here, Turner managed to get Cook to blurt out a key detail, which weakened Cook's reliability as a witness.

The prosecution then called Ira Strickland, Jr., the former owner of the Bay Harbor Poolroom, as a witness. Strickland testified about what he had seen when he arrived at the pool room on the morning of the break-in. He also told the court that Gideon had occasionally worked at the pool room. Gideon wasn't authorized to be there on the morning of the crime. The taxi driver who picked up Gideon on the morning of the crime testified next. When questioned by Turner, he stated that he had not noticed Gideon's pockets bulging with change. The prosecution rested its case.

Turner called J.D. Henderson, a local grocer, as his first witness. Henderson testified that, on the morning of the crime, Cook came into his store. He told the grocer that "the law had picked him up for questioning" and said that he saw someone in the pool room but was "not sure who it was. He said, 'It looked like Mr. Gideon.'"[87] This was a less positive identification of Gideon than Cook had made during his testimony in court.

Turner then called his client to the witness stand. Gideon testified that he did not break into the pool room. He had called the taxi to go into town to get a drink. He got the change from gambling. He told the jury he had no reason to steal bottles of wine because he didn't drink wine. Turner gave his client one last chance to convince the jury of his innocence:

> *Turner:* What do you say to this charge that you broke and entered the pool hall?
> *Gideon:* I'm not guilty of it—I know nothing about it.[88]

The prosecutor then cross-examined Gideon. He zeroed in on the $25.28 in change in Gideon's pockets. Gideon stuck to his testimony that the coins were his gambling winnings. He said that he sometimes carried as much as $100 in change

February 13, 1963

Dear Hugo:

Re: No. 155 - Gideon V. Cochran

I agree and gladly join your Gideon opinion.

I have just one suggestion. On page 4, in the first sentence of the first paragraph of II after the words, "the Sixth Amendment," you may want to consider elimination of the words, "which originally applied only to trials in federal courts."

I think this anticipates the result and the thought embodied in the words is, of course, fully developed in the opinion.

Cordially,

Mr. Justice Black

The document above is a memo written on February 13, 1963, by Justice Arthur Goldberg suggesting an adjustment to the language of Hugo Black's decision.

because he didn't want to leave that much cash in his hotel room. It wouldn't be safe. When Gideon stepped off the witness stand, all the testimony in the trial had been given. In his closing statement, Turner focused on Henry Cook. He told the jury:

This probationer [Cook] has been out at a dance drinking beer . . . He does a peculiar thing [when he supposedly sees Gideon inside the pool room]. He doesn't call the police, he doesn't notify the owner, he just walked to the corner and walked back [as Cook had testified]. . . . What happened to the beer and wine and the Cokes? I'll tell you—[they were] left there in that old model Chevrolet [the car driven by Cook's friends]. The beer ran out at midnight in Apalachicola. . . . Why was Cook walking back and forth? I'll give you the explanation: He was the lookout.[89]

Turner then turned the jury's attention to Gideon. He admitted that his client was a gambler and that he had been drinking whiskey that morning. But he had a different explanation for Gideon's actions than the prosecutor: "I submit to you that he did just what he said that morning—he walked out of his hotel and went to that telephone booth [to call the cab]," Turner stated. "Cook saw him, and here was a perfect answer for Cook [when questioned by the police]. He names Gideon."[90]

The prosecutor summarized the testimony for the jury. He stressed the amount of change in Gideon's pocket:

> Twenty-five dollars' worth of change, that's a lot to carry in your pockets. But Mr. Gideon carried one hundred dollars' worth of change in his pocket. Do you believe that? There's no evidence here of any animosity by Cook toward Gideon. There's no evidence here that Cook and his friends took this beer and wine.[91]

The judge instructed the jury that they must believe Gideon guilty beyond a reasonable doubt in order to convict him. Turner had requested that the judge use that specific language in his instructions. The jury filed out of the courtroom at 4:20 P.M to deliberate. An hour later, they returned. The court clerk read their verdict: not guilty.

McCrary had written of Gideon's first trial: "In my opinion, he did as well as most lawyers could have done in handling his case."[92] After his second trial, it was clear that Gideon had not done as well as Fred Turner. The attorney had the necessary legal training, courtroom experience, and knowledge of the community to present a successful defense for his client. Gideon's insistence that Turner serve as his lawyer may have been the decisive factor in his acquittal. The high-powered Miami lawyers may not have been able to investigate the crime or persuade the local jury as effectively as Turner.

5 The Right to Counsel After *Gideon*

In *Gideon v. Wainwright*, the Supreme Court ruled that having a lawyer was an essential part of a fair trial for defendants charged with a serious crime. In many cases following *Gideon*, the Court considered whether criminal defendants had the constitutional right to the assistance of legal counsel at other stages of the criminal justice system. They also considered whether the right to counsel extended to other types of legal hearings. The Court also reviewed cases involving other right to counsel issues, including whether defendants had the right of self-representation and the right to effective counsel.

THE RIGHT TO COUNSEL BEFORE TRIAL

One year after their decision in *Gideon*, the Court considered a case in which a suspect arrested for murder repeatedly asked to speak with his lawyer before answering any police questions. They refused each request, even though the suspect's lawyer was at the police station demanding to see his client. The detectives hoped to get a get a confession. The arrestee, Danny Escobedo, eventually gave in and answered their questions about the murder. He made several statements that were later used against him in his trial. Escobedo was convicted, and his attorney appealed the case to the Supreme Court. Escobedo's lawyer argued that the Sixth Amendment required the police to allow a suspect to consult with his lawyer. In *Escobedo v. Illinois* (1964), the Court overturned Escobedo's conviction. It stressed the need for legal counsel when the police's criminal investigation changes into a criminal accusation. Writing for the Court, Justice Arthur Goldberg asserted,

> We hold only that when the process shifts from investigatory to accusatory—when its focus is on the accused and its purpose is to elicit a confession—our adversary system begins to operate, and, under the circumstances here, the accused must be permitted to consult with his lawyer.[93]

In other words, the right to counsel begins once the police focus their investigation on an individual and the purpose of the police questioning is to get the person to confess to the crime. Thus, *Escobedo* extended the right to counsel from the trial stage to the interrogation phase.

In another case involving lawyers in the interrogation room, the Court faced the issue of whether the Constitution required police to inform suspects of their constitutional rights to remain silent and to have an attorney present during questioning. Ernesto Miranda had been convicted of rape in a Phoenix,

Danny Escobedo, pictured at work in 1966, was given his freedom when his murder confession was ruled invalid by the Supreme Court in *Escobedo v. Illinois*. The case served as a precedent for others, including *Miranda v. Arizona*.

Arizona, court. Before consulting an attorney, he had signed a confession in which he admitted committing the crime. In appealing the conviction, Miranda's attorney argued that his client had been denied a fair trial. It was just as important for the accused to have legal counsel during police questioning as it was during trial. He stressed that Miranda would not have confessed if a lawyer had been present in the police interrogation room to advise him of his right to remain silent. By a narrow 5–4 vote, the Court ruled in *Miranda v. Arizona* (1966) that the use of Miranda's confession as evidence had violated his Fifth Amendment rights. The Fifth Amendment of the Constitution guarantees that no citizen "shall be compelled in any criminal case to be a witness against himself."[94] In other words, criminal defendants have the right not to testify against themselves in a court of law. This right is commonly known as the right to remain silent.

The Court ruled in *Miranda* that statements made by a person accused of a crime could not be used as evidence at his or her trial unless the accused "voluntarily, knowingly, and intelligently"[95] waived the constitutional right to remain silent. The Court provided police guidelines to follow. Before questioning suspects, police officers had to inform them of their rights. They had the right to remain silent. Anything they said could be used against them in a court of law. They had the right to the presence of an attorney. If they could not afford an attorney, one would be appointed prior to any questioning. A suspect could waive, or give up, any of these rights, as long as it was a voluntary decision. Once suspects state that they understand their Miranda rights and waive them, any statements they make will usually be admissible in court.

In the *Miranda* case, four justices strongly disagreed, arguing that Miranda had voluntarily confessed. They warned that having lawyers in the interrogation room would "discourage any confession at all."[96] Three of the dissenting justices stated that the decision had little support in previous Court decisions and required "a strained reading of [the] history" of the Fifth

Amendment.[97] Law enforcement officials and many politicians and citizens agreed. They worried that *Miranda* would handcuff police in their efforts to persuade suspects to confess. Fewer confessions would lead to few convictions and more criminals on the street.

Miranda was a groundbreaking and controversial decision. It extended the right to remain silent beyond the courtroom and into the police interrogation room. At the time *Escobedo* and *Miranda* were decided, police commonly used psychological pressure—and sometimes physical intimidation—to

 THE MIRANDA WARNING

"You have the right to remain silent. If you give up the right to remain silent, anything you say can and will be used against you in a court of law. You have the right to an attorney. If you desire an attorney but cannot afford one, an attorney will be obtained for you before police questioning."

Most people are familiar with this speech, often heard on TV police dramas. Law enforcement officers throughout the United States recite this speech, or one similar to it, to suspects before questioning them about specific crimes. This speech is known as the Miranda warning because its requirements were established in the 1966 Supreme Court case *Miranda v. Arizona*.

As a result of *Miranda*, police investigators are required to notify suspects of their rights to silence and to legal counsel before they can begin questioning. Notification has to be made at the moment the person can reasonably be considered a suspect under interrogation, even if it is before an arrest. If at any stage in the interrogation a detained suspect indicates that he or she wants to consult with a lawyer, the questioning must stop. If the person declines to be interrogated, the questioning must stop. Any evidence gained in violation of *Miranda* will be inadmissible at trial.

obtain confessions. To increase the certainty that a defendant's confession had been voluntary, the Court created a new procedure. Police must notify all arrestees of their constitutional rights before they can begin questioning them. This notification became known as the Miranda warning.

In *United States v. Wade* (1967), the Court considered whether the right to counsel should be extended to lineups. A lineup is a police procedure in which an eyewitness has the opportunity to identify a suspect from a group of people standing in a line. In *Wade*, the defendant had been arrested for a bank robbery in Texas. Before trial, an FBI agent held a lineup that included Wade and several other prisoners. The agent did not notify Wade's attorney. Two bank employees fingered Wade as the robber. Writing for the Court, Justice William Brennan concluded that Wade's "counsel should have been notified of the impending lineup, and counsel's presence should have been a requisite to conduct of the lineup."[98] The court based its decision on the fact that, like a confession, a lineup identification is a powerful piece of evidence. By being present at the lineup, the suspect's attorney can make sure that it is conducted fairly and that the suspect's rights are not violated. In *Moore v. Illinois* (1977), the Court extended the right to counsel to a one-person lineup, in which a witness is shown the suspect only and asked whether he or she is the perpetrator.

In *Coleman v. Alabama* (1970), the Court extended the right to counsel to preliminary hearings. The defendant had appeared at a pretrial hearing to determine whether there was enough evidence to indict him on a charge of attempted murder. Coleman did not have an attorney to represent him at the hearing. The Court held that, like the interrogation phase, the preliminary hearing is a critical stage in the criminal justice process. Writing for the Court, Justice Brennan noted, "the guiding hand of counsel at the preliminary hearing is essential to protect the indigent accused against an erroneous or improper prosecution."[99] In two other cases that same year, *Brady v. United States*

Ernesto Miranda (*right*) walks with his attorney, John Flynn, in 1966. Miranda's landmark case resulted in the institution of the so-called Miranda warning, which police officers must read to suspects upon arrest.

(1970) and *McMann v. Richardson* (1970), the Court extended the right to counsel to plea negotiations. A plea negotiation occurs when a prosecutor offers to allow an accused person to plead guilty to a lesser offense. In some cases, an accused person will accept the terms of a plea bargain in order to avoid a trial for a crime that would likely result in a stiffer sentence.

THE RIGHT TO COUNSEL AT TRIAL

The *Gideon* decision left many questions about the scope of the right to counsel at trial unanswered. *Gideon* made clear that poor defendants in all felony cases were entitled to the appointment of legal counsel, but what about defendants charged with misdemeanors under state laws? In *Argersinger v. Hamlin* (1972), the Court held that the Sixth and Fourteenth amendments required the appointment of counsel in any misdemeanor case in which imprisonment could be imposed.

The Court later clarified its *Argersinger* rule in *Scott v. Illinois* (1979). At trial, the defendant had been convicted of shoplifting and fined $50. He appealed his conviction, arguing that the Sixth and Fourteenth amendments and *Argersinger* required the Illinois court to appoint counsel to represent him. Writing for the Court, Chief Justice William Rehnquist disagreed, stating,

> The Sixth and Fourteenth Amendments require that no indigent criminal defendant be sentenced to a term of imprisonment unless the State has afforded him the right to assistance of appointed counsel in his defense, but do not require a state trial court to appoint counsel for a criminal defendant, such as petitioner, who is charged with a statutory offense for which imprisonment upon conviction is authorized but not imposed.[100]

As a result of *Scott*, if a trial judge believes that imprisonment is a possible sentence, the Constitution requires him or her to appoint counsel. If the judge believes that a guilty verdict will result in a form of punishment besides imprisonment, such as a fine, the Constitution does not require the appointment of counsel.

THE RIGHT TO COUNSEL IN OTHER SETTINGS

The Supreme Court has extended the right to counsel to legal proceedings other than trials. In the case *In re Gault* (1967), 15-year-old Gerald Gault was arrested for making lewd telephone calls. (*In re* is the Latin phrase for "in the matter of." The term is used in legal cases that do not have opposing parties.) At a later hearing, a juvenile court judge committed Gault "as a juvenile delinquent to the State Industrial School 'for the period of his minority [that is, until age 21], unless sooner discharged by due process of law.'"[101] Gault appealed his commitment, arguing that the juvenile court should have provided him with legal counsel. Writing for the Court, Justice Abe Fortas asserted,

> A proceeding where the issue is whether the child will be found to be delinquent and subjected to the loss of his liberty for years is comparable in seriousness to a felony prosecution. The juvenile needs the assistance of counsel to cope with problems of law, to make skilled inquiry into the facts, to insist upon regularity of the proceedings, and to ascertain whether he has a defense and to prepare and submit it.[102]

Thus, states must provide counsel to juveniles in delinquency hearings who cannot afford to hire their own lawyer.

The Court later extended the right to counsel to various other legal proceedings. The right to counsel now applies to mental competency and commitment hearings. It also applies to legal proceedings involving family law matters, such as nonpayment of support, child dependency, and abuse and neglect. The right to counsel also applies to extradition hearings. Extradition hearings determine whether an accused or convicted person should be transferred to the location in which the crime is alleged to have been committed. The transfer can be from one country to another or from one state to another. In each of these cases, the Court noted that whenever the government seeks to affect basic rights, the fairness of the hearing depends on counsel being provided to poor defendants.

THE RIGHT TO COUNSEL AFTER CONVICTION

The Supreme Court has also extended the right to appointed counsel to postconviction legal proceedings. In *Douglas v. California* (1963), the Court held that convicts have the right to appointed counsel to handle the appeal of their convictions. In *United States v. Tucker* (1972), the court affirmed the right to counsel during sentencing proceedings. The Court has also ruled that the right to counsel applies to some prison disciplinary proceedings and some probation and parole hearings.

OTHER ISSUES INVOLVING THE RIGHT TO COUNSEL

The Supreme Court has further defined the reach of the right to counsel in cases involving retained counsel, the right of self-representation, and the effectiveness of appointed counsel.

The Right to Retained Counsel

The Court has ruled that the Sixth Amendment provides defendants with an absolute right to hire the counsel of their choice. In *Chandler v. Fretag* (1954), the defendant had appeared in court without a lawyer to plead guilty to a burglary charge. At the hearing, he was informed for the first time that he would be considered a habitual criminal because of his prior felony convictions. As a result, the conviction in this case would result in a sentence of life imprisonment. He asked for a continuance (court-approved delay) in order to consult with an attorney, but the court denied his request. The Supreme Court overturned his conviction. Writing for the Court, Chief Justice Earl Warren stated,

> Regardless of whether petitioner would have been entitled to the appointment of counsel, his right to be heard through his own counsel was unqualified. . . . A necessary corollary is that a defendant must be given a reasonable opportunity to employ and consult with counsel; otherwise, the right to be heard by counsel would be of little worth.[103]

Another issue involving retained counsel occurs when a lawyer is defending two or more defendants in the same case. If the lawyer tells the trial judge that he cannot provide effective legal counsel to each of his clients because of possible conflicts of interest between his clients, the judge in most cases must allow the defendants to hire separate counsel. If the court has appointed the attorney, the trial judge must appoint a lawyer for each defendant.

The Right to Represent Oneself

Gideon involved a defendant who requested a lawyer to represent him. What about defendants who want to represent themselves? Can they turn down a court's appointment of counsel? A 1975 case raised the issue of whether the constitutional right to counsel was satisfied when a criminal defendant voluntarily decided to represent himself. In *Faretta v. California*, the defendant was charged with grand theft. At his arraignment, the trial judge, following the directive of *Gideon*, assigned the local public defender office to represent him. Faretta, however, asked to represent himself. He asserted that he had once represented himself in a criminal prosecution and that he had a high school education. He did not want to be represented by the public defender because he believed that the lawyer was overloaded with cases. The judge accepted Faretta's waiver of counsel. At a later hearing, however, the judge reversed his earlier ruling. He stated that, on further consideration, Faretta had no constitutional right to defend himself. The judge appointed the public defender to represent him. A jury later convicted Faretta.

In overturning Faretta's conviction, the Supreme Court recognized a criminal defendant's Sixth Amendment right to conduct his own defense. The Court ruled that in order to represent himself, the accused must knowingly and intelligently waive the benefits of the right to legal counsel. Writing for the Court, Justice Potter Stewart noted, "the right to self-representation—to make one's own defense personally—is . . . necessarily implied by the structure of the [Sixth] Amendment. The right to defend is given directly to the accused; for it is he who suffers the consequences if the defense fails."[104] The court warned that defendants who represent themselves could not later complain that the poor quality of their own defense had denied them effective assistance of counsel.

The Court described the essential elements of self-representation in a later case, *McKaskle v. Wiggins* (1984). This case involved the rights of a self-represented defendant when the trial court had appointed a "standby counsel." Wiggins appealed his conviction, claiming that the standby counsel had caused him to lose the case. Writing for the Court, Justice Sandra Day O'Connor asserted that a defendant representing himself "must be allowed to control the organization and content of his own defense, to make motions, to argue points of law, to participate in voir dire [jury selection], to question witnesses, and to address the court and the jury at appropriate points in the trial."[105] The Court ruled that the participation of the standby lawyer in Wiggins's trial did not violate his Sixth Amendment rights. The trial transcript showed that the court-appointed lawyer had not hindered Wiggins's presentation of his defense.

Effective Assistance of Counsel

The most controversial right-to-counsel cases following *Gideon* have been those involving effective assistance of counsel. As the number of criminal cases handled by appointed counsel grew, an increasing number of convicts began appealing their cases on the grounds of incompetent counsel. In 1980, the Supreme Court stated in *Cuyler v. Sullivan* that "[t]he right to counsel prevents the States from conducting trials at which persons who face incarceration must defend themselves without adequate legal assistance."[106] In *Strickland v. Washington* (1984), the Supreme Court affirmed that defendants were entitled to effective counsel during criminal proceedings. The case provided a test to determine whether counsel in criminal trials or capital sentencing hearings had been ineffective. The first part of the *Strickland* test focused on attorney performance. Had the attorney been unsatisfactory? The second part of the test focused on whether the outcome of the trial had been affected. Was the attorney's performance so bad that it may have changed the result?

In order to establish ineffective counsel under the *Strickland* rule, a defendant "must show that there is a reasonable probability that, but for counsel's unprofessional errors, the result of the proceeding would have been different. A reasonable probability is a probability sufficient to undermine confidence in the outcome."[107] In *Strickland*, the defendant proved neither part of the test. Strickland had claimed he received the death penalty because his attorney did not introduce character and psychological evidence during a postconviction hearing. The hearing determined whether the death penalty should be imposed. The Supreme Court noted that Strickland's lawyer had not introduced the evidence because it would allow the prosecutor to introduce evidence of the defendant's past criminal convictions. The Court concluded that the attorney's decision was "the result of reasonable professional judgment."[108] Furthermore, the Court concluded that Strickland had failed to prove any prejudice on his attorney's part because it was reasonable to assume that the evidence of the defendant's past crimes would have outweighed the evidence of good character that his attorney could have presented.

The Court eventually made the *Strickland* test stricter in *Lockhart v. Fretwell* (1993). "In order to established ineffective counsel under *Strickland*," Chief Justice William Rehnquist wrote for the 7–2 majority, "a defendant must demonstrate that counsel's errors are so serious as to deprive him of a trial whose result is unfair or unreliable, . . . not merely that the outcome would have been different."[109]

Defendants now have a very difficult time establishing that their convictions should be overturned because of ineffective counsel. Following the Supreme Court's instructions in *Strickland* that "judicial scrutiny of counsel's performance must be highly deferential,"[110] appeals courts are reluctant to rule that ineffective counsel caused an unfair or unreliable result in a

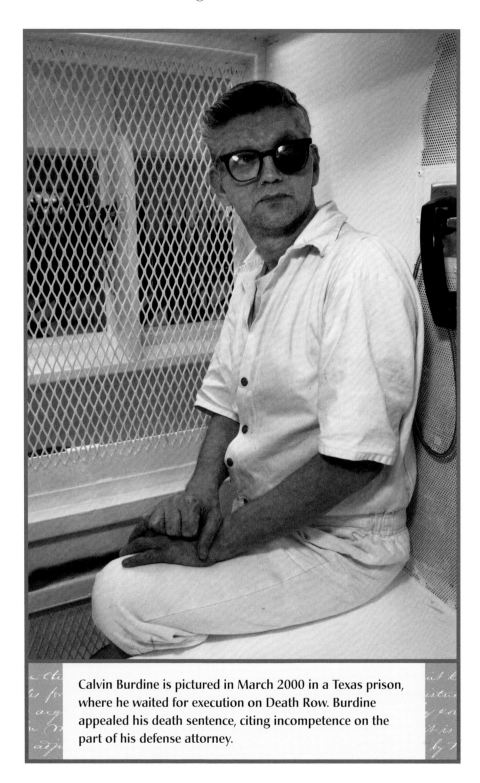

Calvin Burdine is pictured in March 2000 in a Texas prison, where he waited for execution on Death Row. Burdine appealed his death sentence, citing incompetence on the part of his defense attorney.

criminal trial. Appeals courts almost never second-question the strategic choices made by trial lawyers.

In 2002, the Supreme Court declined to grant certiorari in a widely publicized case involving ineffective counsel. In 1984, a Houston, Texas, jury convicted Calvin Burdine of murder. He received the death penalty. Burdine appealed his conviction. He argued that his trial was unfair because his court-appointed lawyer slept through substantial parts of the trial. Burdine's case took nearly 20 years to resolve. He received six stays (delays) of execution while waiting for the final outcome of his appeal.

In 1999, a U.S. district judge ruled that Burdine's sleeping lawyer was essentially the same as having no lawyer at all. He overturned Burdine's conviction, granting him a new trial. The State of Texas appealed. One year later, a three-judge panel of the U.S. Court of Appeals for the Fifth Circuit upheld the original conviction, ruling that despite repeatedly falling asleep, Burdine's lawyer provided him with effective legal counsel. The 3-judge panel's ruling was later overturned by a 14-judge panel of the same U.S. Court of Appeals by a vote of 9–5. The lawyer handling Burdine's appeal, Robert McGlasson, expressed his shock at the vote. He stated, "The inexplicable result is where five appellate court judges can reach the conclusion that the Sixth Amendment's right to counsel doesn't mean that the lawyer has to be awake."[111]

The State of Texas appealed the 9–5 ruling of the court of appeals. On June 3, 2002, the U.S. Supreme Court declined to hear the case. By rejecting the state's appeal, the decision of the court of appeals was final. Burdine's new trial was scheduled for August 2003. Two months before the trial date, Burdine accepted a plea bargain. Not wanting to face the possibility of a death sentence again, he agreed to plea guilty to murder and accept a sentence of life in prison.

The Future of the Right to Counsel

6

Gideon v. Wainwright marked the turning point in the constitutional right to counsel. Beginning in 1963, defendants in all felony trials were guaranteed counsel, even if they could not afford to hire a lawyer. *Gideon* was a key step in the evolution of the right to counsel. The Court's decision, however, did not resolve all the problems associated with the right to counsel. Not everyone gets a lawyer as committed and skilled as Fred Turner, who represented Gideon in his second trial. The system of free legal defense that arose as a result of the *Gideon* case has been plagued with inadequate funding, overworked lawyers, and poor-quality legal representation.

THE EFFECT OF *GIDEON* ON DEFENDANTS

In *Gideon*, the Supreme Court affirmed that the Sixth Amendment guaranteed criminal defendants in felony cases the right to an attorney. If a defendant could not afford an attorney, the Sixth Amendment required the court to appoint legal counsel. Later cases established that the right to counsel applied to many legal proceedings besides felony trials. As noted in Chapter 5, the Supreme Court has ruled that legal counsel is also required for misdemeanor cases in which imprisonment will be the punishment upon conviction. In addition, the Court has held that legal representation is also required for pretrial hearings, such as arraignments, as well as postconviction hearings, such as appeals.

THE EFFECT OF *GIDEON* ON FEDERAL, STATE, AND LOCAL GOVERNMENTS

Gideon mandated that courts across the country appoint counsel for defendants who cannot afford to hire their own attorney. This placed both administrative and financial burdens on the courts and other governmental agencies. Because of the earlier case *Johnson v. Zerbst* (1938), the federal government already had in place a basic system for providing lawyers for indigent defendants when *Gideon* was decided. The majority of states also had created some type of system to provide court-appointed counsel by 1963. Other states, including Gideon's home state of Florida, needed to create brand new systems.

In the four decades since *Gideon*, federal and state government officials, legal scholars, prosecutors, and defense attorneys have worked together to create national guidelines and standards for indigent defense. In 1974, the National Legal Aid and Defender Association began a nationwide study of criminal defense services for the poor. Their 560-page report, *Guidelines for Legal Defense Systems* (1976), provided approaches and procedures that help federal and state governments meet

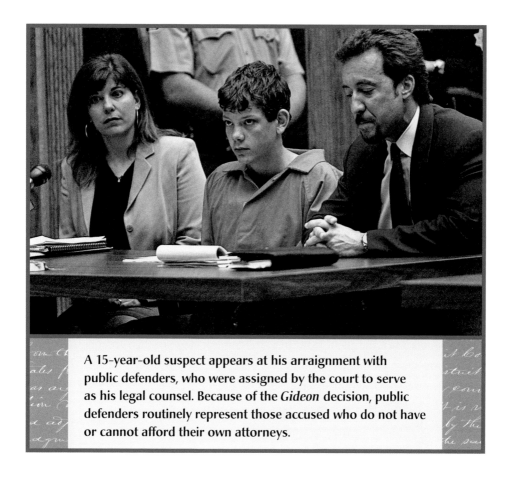

A 15-year-old suspect appears at his arraignment with public defenders, who were assigned by the court to serve as his legal counsel. Because of the *Gideon* decision, public defenders routinely represent those accused who do not have or cannot afford their own attorneys.

the defense needs of the nation's indigent population. The guidelines covered a wide range of topics, from the types of cases in which counsel should be provided to the points in the legal process at which counsel should be present. They also discussed the financial eligibility of defendants, the administrative structures of public defenders offices, sources for funding, and appropriate fees for appointed counsel.

Some state governments have assumed the responsibility for indigent defense. Their legislatures have established statewide agencies to provide legal representation to poor defendants and have also provided funding for them. Other states have left it up to the counties to set up and pay for indigent defense programs.

Three major types of indigent defense models have evolved. The first type is the public defender model. Many states and counties have established government agencies, known as public defender offices, that employ attorneys, investigators, and other legal professions. Many criminal law experts believe the public

HOW DOES AN ATTORNEY ASSIST A DEFENDANT?

The defense attorney plays a critical role in almost every criminal case. The actual work of an attorney varies from case to case, depending on the criminal charges involved and the circumstances of the case. The criminal defense lawyer protects the rights and interests of the client from the arraignment stage to the sentencing stage (in the event of a guilty verdict). Criminal defense attorneys have several responsibilities:

- Advising the defendant of his or her rights and explaining what to expect at different stages of the criminal process
- Negotiating plea bargain offers from the prosecutor and counseling the client about whether to accept the offer
- Investigating all the facts and evidence related to the case and lining up witnesses and experts for the defense
- At trial, cross-examining prosecution witnesses, objecting to improper questions and evidence, and presenting all relevant legal defenses on behalf of the defendant
- Ensuring that the defendant's constitutional rights are not violated by law enforcement officials or during court proceedings

defender model is the most effective one. In the other two models, trial courts appoint private lawyers to represent the poor. In one appointment system, lawyers volunteer to be placed on a list of available attorneys, and the state or county pays these attorneys a set rate for representing indigent defendants. In the other appointment system, the state or county negotiates a bulk contract with a legal services company. This company then provides lawyers to represent poor defendants. Some states have a mixed system with, for example, public defender offices in heavily populated counties and a court-appointment system in less populated counties.

Over time, the systems for providing legal counsel to the poor evolved. Encouraging progress was made, but action varied regarding the Supreme Court's promise in *Gideon* of a fair trial for all defendants. Some members of the legal community joined civil rights organizations in pointing out that the indigent defense standards adopted by some states or counties were not implemented. These standards merely appeared on paper but were not carried out in the courts. Many public defender offices were overwhelmed with cases. Their funding did not keep pace with the funding for prosecutors' offices. Bulk contracts for court-appointed lawyers were awarded to the lowest bidders. The quality of the legal service provided by these companies was often ignored. The case-by-case appointment of counsel system placed a heavy burden on local attorneys. Cases were often assigned to less busy—and perhaps poorly qualified—lawyers.

The effects of all these problems soon became evident. The quality of legal representation for the poor was often very bad. In the worst cases, it seemed to some observers that inadequate representation was about the same as no representation at all. The number of appeals filed by convicts claiming ineffective counsel increased. The legitimacy of some criminal convictions were called into question, which reflected poorly on the criminal justice system.

In 1997, the U.S. Department of Justice hosted a national conference. Leaders of the indigent defense community discussed ways in which the federal government could help local governments establish stronger, more stable indigent defense systems. The conference's report, *Improving Criminal Justice Systems Through Expanded Strategies and Innovative Collaborations* (2000), addressed many of the problems under the current system, including quality of legal services and attorney workloads. It noted:

> Although our Constitution guarantees defendants the right to a lawyer in criminal cases, the implementation

PUBLIC DEFENDER OFFICES

Many states and counties have established public defender offices to handle the legal representation of indigent defendants. The public defender offices in Wisconsin and Colorado, for example, are independent agencies that are part of those states' executive branches. In contrast, in other states, such as California and Florida, public defender offices are county agencies.

Public defender offices represent anyone who has been accused of a crime and cannot afford to hire a private lawyer. Defendants requesting free legal representation are typically assigned an attorney. Courts, however, generally require defendants to show that they qualify for the services of public defender offices. They must complete a financial statement showing their income, savings, and expenses. Some defendants end up paying all or part of the costs for their legal defense. Those who show that they cannot afford to pay are not required to reimburse the public defenders office.

of this constitutional right is applied unevenly across the nation. The Bureau of Justice Statistics reports that in 1992, nearly 80 percent of defendants charged with felonies in the nation's 75 largest counties relied on a public defender or assigned counsel for legal representation. But too many jurisdictions lack the financial capital—or the political will—to provide adequate funding, staffing, training, and access to technology that can establish guilt or innocence such as DNA analysis, and other resources to ensure that every defendant receives effective assistance of counsel.[112]

The document also proposed new standards, covering such issues as ensuring attorney qualifications, monitoring attorney performance, and providing continued legal training. It recommended the maximum number of cases a lawyer should take on, how the budgets for indigent defense systems should compare to prosecution budgets, and ways to ensure that indigent defender systems could be protected from undue political forces.

In 2003, the legal community celebrated the fortieth anniversary of *Gideon v. Wainwright*. Legal scholars and journalists reflected on the impact of *Gideon*. They compared the status of the right to counsel for indigent defendants in 2003 to the days before Gideon's case. The contemporary conditions that they described were alarming. An editorial in the *New York Times* on March 23, 2003, noted, "the reality is that for many defendants, the promise of *Gideon* has been hollow. Poor people are still imprisoned, and even put to death, after trials in which they have shockingly inadequate legal representation."[113] The editorial continued:

> *Gideon* laid out a constitutional principle, but it is up to the states to apply it. Their programs are woefully inadequate. In many of the 22 states that pay for such legal services entirely at the state level, the level of financing is so low that lawyers cannot afford to investigate and prepare proper defenses.

In the 28 states that rely on local financing, the quality of representation is even worse. In some Texas counties, defendants wait months in jail before seeing a lawyer. In Georgia, some counties try indigent defendants in nonfelony cases without providing lawyers, even when a conviction may result in prison time—a direct violation of *Gideon*.

The recent spate of exonerations based on DNA tests has demonstrated that inadequate representation can, and does, lead to wrongful convictions. A Montana man, speaking at an Open Society Institute panel this month, told of spending 15 years in prison on a sexual assault charge after a trial in which his court-appointed lawyer did no investigation, hired no experts and failed to file an appeal. After 15 years, he was cleared with DNA evidence.[114]

The editorial went on to recommend that the states need to make sure that attorneys are not overwhelmed by their caseloads, and that there should be sufficient resources for investigators and expert witnesses. It recommended that states set up professional public defender offices or make sure independent attorneys are trained and supervised.

A March 24, 2003, news article in the *Atlanta Journal-Constitution* made similar points. It noted:

Although there have been steady gains in some areas of legal representation for the poor, the promise of *Gideon* remains largely unfulfilled today.

In Georgia, indigent defendants are still herded through the criminal justice system without the benefit of a lawyer to assist them. In counties such as Coweta just southwest of Atlanta or Crisp in south Georgia, judges routinely instruct lawyerless defendants to talk directly with prosecutors and resolve their cases.

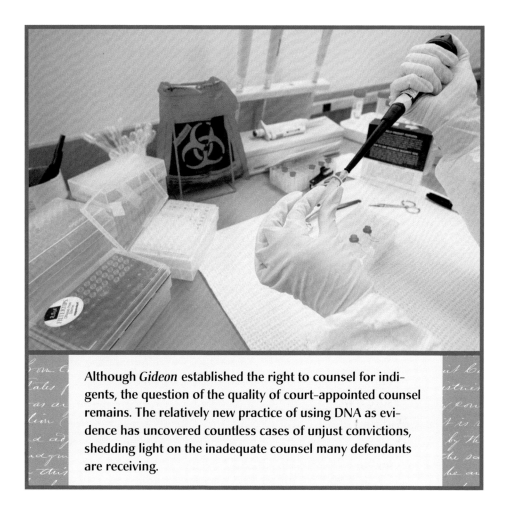

Although *Gideon* established the right to counsel for indigents, the question of the quality of court-appointed counsel remains. The relatively new practice of using DNA as evidence has uncovered countless cases of unjust convictions, shedding light on the inadequate counsel many defendants are receiving.

Across the state, thousands of poor defendants are represented by overwhelmed, underfunded attorneys unable to investigate their cases or spend any time on them. Many attorneys do little more than process their clients through court.

"We see criminal defendants languishing in jail for days, weeks and even months at a time without even knowing who their appointed lawyer is, much less getting a visit from them," said John Cole Vodicka, whose Americus-based Prison & Jail Project monitors courts in southwest Georgia.[115]

The article noted that the problems were widespread. Non-violent cases in Oregon were being dismissed because the local indigent defense system was inadequately funded. In one California county, more than 10,000 defendants a year were pleading guilty to crimes without ever speaking with an attorney. The attorneys in public defender offices in two Florida counties were handling more than five times the recommended number of cases each year. In Mississippi, one county had sued the state, claiming that it was the state's duty to provide the funds for indigent defense.

That same year, the Georgetown University Law Center in Washington, D.C., hosted a conference to mark the anniversary of *Gideon v. Wainwright*. Abe Krash, who helped Abe Fortas prepare Gideon's appeal, spoke about the case.

> It's difficult to recapture the spirit of idealism that infected us at the time. Unfortunately, some things were not apparent to us at that time. It's not enough to say you're entitled to a lawyer. You need to have a competent lawyer, one that has to be provided adequate funds to retain experts and investigators to conduct an adequate defense.[116]

Krash expressed his hope that the goal of having well-funded indigent defense programs in every county would be realized before *Gideon*'s fiftieth anniversary.

THE LEGACY OF CLARENCE EARL GIDEON

After the jury in his second trial found him not guilty, Clarence Earl Gideon spoke with reporters on the courthouse steps. That night he visited the Bay Harbor Poolroom. He borrowed a few dollars from a friend. A newspaper reporter asked him, "Do you feel like you accomplished something?" Gideon responded, "Well, I did."[117] Although his case received widespread media coverage, Gideon quickly faded from the public limelight. He died in Fort Lauderdale, Florida,

Clarence Earl Gideon was buried in an unmarked grave in Hannibal, Missouri. Thirteen years later, a local branch of the ACLU donated this tombstone inscribed with a worthy tribute to Gideon's importance in U.S. history.

on January 18, 1972, at age 61. His remains were sent to his relatives in Hannibal, Missouri. They buried him in an unmarked grave.

Today, Gideon is remembered for making a simple plea that a criminal trial was not fair unless the defendant had a lawyer. By demanding justice, he changed the law and the administration of justice in the United States. The *Improving Criminal Justice Systems Through Expanded Strategies and Innovative Collaborations* report noted that "[t]he rule of law and our adversarial system demand that one side in the justice process not be fundamentally disadvantaged by a lack of resources. The scales of justice must be balanced if we are to overcome the common perception—held by about 90 percent of Americans according to an American Bar Association poll—that you get only as much justice as you can afford."[118] The right to counsel—for the poor as well as the rich—is essential to ensure justice in criminal cases. In order for the public to have confidence in the nation's legal system, criminal trials should produce fair, reliable results.

Thirteen years after Gideon's death, a Missouri chapter of the American Civil Liberties Union, the civil rights organization that argued on his behalf as a friend of Court, placed a headstone on his grave. It was engraved with a sentence from Clarence Earl Gideon's letter to Abe Fortas. The headstone reads, "Each era finds an improvement in law for the benefit of mankind."[119]

Chronology

1791	The Bill of Rights, which includes the Sixth Amendment's guarantee of the right to counsel, is adopted.
1853	In *Webb v. Baird*, the Indiana Supreme Court recognizes the right of a poor defendant to an attorney at public expense.
1868	The Fourteenth Amendment is ratified. It forbids states from depriving anyone of "life, liberty, or property, without due process of law."
1896	New York Legal Aid Society begins providing legal representation to the poor.
1910	Clarence Earl Gideon and Abe Fortas are born.
1914	Los Angeles starts the first publicly funded legal aid organization.
1932	In *Powell v. Alabama*, the U.S. Supreme Court holds that counsel is required in all state capital trials.
1938	In *Johnson v. Zerbst*, the Supreme Court rules that the Sixth Amendment requires appointment of counsel in federal trials for criminal defendants who cannot afford to hire a lawyer.
1942	In *Betts v. Brady*, the Supreme Court holds that the Sixth Amendment does not guarantee the right to counsel in noncapital state court trials.
1961	Gideon is arrested for and convicted of a Panama City, Florida, burglary. The Florida Supreme Court rejects Gideon's request for a writ of habeas corpus.
1962	Gideon submits his writ of certiorari and motion to proceed *in forma pauperis* to the U.S. Supreme Court. The Court agrees to hear Gideon's appeal and appoints Abe Fortas to serve as his appellate lawyer.

1963   The Supreme Court hears oral argument and an-
        nounces its decision in *Gideon v. Wainwright*. The
        Court rules that a poor person is entitled to the ap-
        pointment of defense counsel in state felony trials.
        At Gideon's retrial on the burglary charges, the jury
        returns a not-guilty verdict.

1966   In *Miranda v. Arizona*, the Supreme Court rules that
        statements made by a person accused of a crime could
        not be used as evidence at his or her trial unless the
        accused "voluntarily, knowingly, and intelligently"
        waived their constitutional right to remain silent.

1972   In *Argersinger v. Hamlin*, the Supreme Court rules that
        counsel should be appointed to a poor defendant in

Timeline

1896
New York Legal Aid Society
begins providing legal representation to the poor.

1791
The Bill of Rights, which
includes the Sixth
Amendment's guarantee
of the right to counsel,
is adopted.

1791 *hird.... Congress shall make no law respecting an* **1938**

1938
In *Johnson v. Zerbst*, the Supreme Court rules that the
Sixth Amendment requires
appointment of counsel in
federal trials for criminal defendants who cannot afford
to hire a lawyer.

1868
The Fourteenth Amendment is ratified. It forbids states from depriving
anyone of "life, liberty, or property,
without due process of law."

any misdemeanor case in which imprisonment could be imposed.

1984   In *Strickland v. Washington*, the Supreme Court rules that defendants are entitled to effective counsel during criminal proceedings.

1997   The U.S. Department of Justice holds a conference to discuss ways in which the federal government can help local governments provide better legal services to poor criminal defendants.

2003   The legal community celebrates the fortieth anniversary of *Gideon v. Wainwright*. Some observers note that the current state of indigent defense systems do not live up to the promise of *Gideon*.

1961
Clarence Earl Gideon is arrested for and convicted of a Panama City, Florida, burglary.

1963
The Supreme Court hears oral argument and announces its decision in *Gideon v. Wainwright*.

1961 **2003**

1962
The Court agrees to hear Gideon's appeal and appoints Abe Fortas to serve as his appellate lawyer.

2003
The legal community celebrates the fortieth anniversary of *Gideon v. Wainwright*.

Notes

Introduction

1. "Amendment XIV." The U.S. Constitution Online. http://www.usconstitution.net/.
2. "Rule 10." Rules of the Supreme Court of the United States. http://www.supremecourtus.gov/ctrules/rulesofthecourt.pdf.
3. Anthony Lewis. *Gideon's Trumpet.* New York: Random House, 1964, p. 10.
4. Ibid., p. 43.

Chapter 1

5. Ibid., p. 67.
6. Ibid., pp. 9–10.
7. Ibid., p. 58.
8. Ibid., p. 59.
9. Ibid., p. 60.
10. Ibid., p. 6.
11. Ibid., p. 33.
12. Ibid., pp. 8–9.
13. Ibid., p. 36.
14. Ibid., pp. 37–38.

Chapter 2

15. "Charter of Privileges Granted by William Penn, esq., to the Inhabitants of Pennsylvania and Territories, October 28, 1701." The Avalon Project at Yale Law School. http://www.yale.edu/lawweb/avalon/states/pa07.htm.
16. "Amendment VI." The U.S. Constitution Online. http://www.usconstitution.net/.
17. "A Century of Lawmaking for a New Nation: U.S. Congressional Documents and Debates, 1774–1875." See Section 29. American Memory: The Library of Congress. http://straylight.law.cornell.edu/usc-cgi/get_external.cgi?type=statRef&target=nonestatnum:1_118.
18. *Johnson v. Zerbst,* 304 U.S. 462 (1938).
19. Ibid., 463.
20. Ibid., 462.
21. 6 Ind.18; quoted in *Betts v. Brady* (1942), 316 U.S. 477.
22. "Amendment XIV." http://www.usconstitution.net/.
23. *Powell v. Alabama,* 287 U.S. 68. (1932).
24. Ibid., 69–70.
25. Ibid., 71.
26. Ibid.
27. *Betts v. Brady,* 316 U.S. 462 (1942).

28. Ibid., 465.
29. Ibid., 471.
30. Ibid., 473.
31. Ibid., 477.
32. Lewis, *Gideon's Trumpet*, p. 112.

Chapter 3
33. Ibid., p. 119.
34. Ibid., p. 120.
35. Ibid., p. 123.
36. *Griffin v. Illinois*, 351 U.S. 17 (1956).
37. Lewis, *Gideon's Trumpet*, p. 126.
38. Ibid., p. 127.
39. Ibid., p. 134.
40. Ibid.
41. Ibid., pp. 134–135.
42. Ibid., p. 135.
43. "Amendment XIV," http://www.usconstitution.net/.
44. *Betts*, 471.
45. Lewis, *Gideon's Trumpet*, p. 136.
46. Ibid., p. 138.
47. Ibid.
48. Ibid., p. 157.
49. Ibid.
50. Ibid., pp. 157–158.
51. Ibid., p. 158.
52. Ibid.
53. Ibid., p. 159.
54. Ibid., pp.159–160.
55. Ibid., p 157.
56. Ibid., p. 142.
57. Ibid., pp. 145–146.
58. Ibid., pp. 149–150.
59. Ibid., pp. 150–151.
60. Ibid., p. 154.

Chapter 4
61. Ibid., p. 167.
62. Ibid., p. 169.
63. Peter Irons and Stephanie Guitton, eds. *May It Please the Court*. New York: New Press, 1993, p. 187.
64. Lewis, *Gideon's Trumpet*, p. 170.
65. Ibid., pp. 170–171.
66. Irons and Guitton, *May It Please the Court*, p. 188.
67. Lewis, *Gideon's Trumpet*, p. 171.
68. Ibid., pp. 171–172.
69. Ibid., p. 173.
70. Ibid., p. 174.
71. Irons and Guitton, *May It Please the Court*, p. 189.
72. Lewis, *Gideon's Trumpet*, discussed ways in which the federal government could help local governments establish stronger, more stable indigent defense systems, p. 167.
73. Ibid., p. 176.
74. Ibid., p. 178.
75. Ibid.
76. Ibid., p. 179.
77. Ibid., p. 180.
78. Ibid., p. 187.
79. *Gideon v. Wainwright*, 372 U.S. 342 (1963).
80. Ibid., 344.
81. Ibid., 345.
82. Lewis, *Gideon's Trumpet*, p. 192.
83. Ibid., p. 226.
84. Ibid., p. 230.

85. Ibid.
86. Ibid., p. 231.
87. Ibid., p. 234.
88. Ibid., p. 235.
89. Ibid., p. 236–237.
90. Ibid., p. 237.
91. Ibid.
92. Ibid., p. 238.

Chapter 5

93. *Escobedo v. Illinois*, 378 U.S. 492 (1964).
94. "Amendment V." http://www.usconstitution.net/.
95. *Miranda v. Arizona*, 384 U.S. 444 (1966).
96. Ibid., 505.
97. Ibid.
98. *United States v. Wade*, 388 U.S. 237 (1967).
99. *Coleman v. Alabama*, 399 U.S. 9 (1970).
100. 440 U.S. 367.
101. *Scott v. Illinois*, 387 U.S. 8 (1979).
102. *Scott*, 36.
103. *Chandler v. Fretag*, 348 U.S. 9–10 (1954).
104. *Faretta v. California*, 422 U.S. 819–820 (1975).
105. *McKaskle v. Wiggins*, 465 U.S. 168 (1984).
106. *Cuyler v. Sullivan*, 446 U.S. 344 (1980).
107. *Strickland v. Washington*, 466 U.S. 669 (1984).
108. Ibid.
109. *Lockhart v. Fretwell*, 506 U.S. 364 (1993).
110. *Strickland*, 669.

111. "Right to Lawyer Still Not a Given for Poor Defendants." National Association of Criminal Defense Lawyers: Gideon at 40: Facing the Crisis, Fulfilling the Promise. From *Atlanta Journal-Constitution*. March 24, 2003. http://www.nacdl.org/public.nsf/GideonAnniversary/news05?opendocument.

Chapter 6

112. National Symposium on Criminal Defense. *Improving Criminal Justice Systems Through Expanded Strategies and Innovative Collaborations*. Washington, D.C.: Government Printing Office, 2000, p. *v*.
113. "Gideon's Trumpet Stilled." National Association of Criminal Defense Lawyers: Gideon at 40: Facing the Crisis, Fulfilling the Promise. From *New York Times*. March 21, 2003. http://www.nacdl.org/public.nsf/GideonAnniversary/news07?opendocument.
114. Ibid.
115. "Right to Lawyer Still Not a Given for Poor Defendants," http://www.nacdl.org/public.nsf/GideonAnniversary/news05?opendocument.

116. Ibid.

117. Lewis, *Gideon's Trumpet,* p. 238.

118. National Symposium on Criminal Defense, *Improving Criminal Justice Systems Through Expanded Strategies and Innovative Collaborations,* p. *v.*

119. Gideon's Gravestone. http://www.nacdl.org/public.nsf/GideonAnniversary/Index1/$FILE/GideonGrave.jpg. Gideon's letter is reproduced in Lewis, *Gideon's Trumpet,* pp. 65–78.

Glossary

amicus curaie   A brief submitted to a court by a person or organization (a "friend of the court") not directly involved in the case.

appeal   A request for a review by a higher court of law of a case previously decided in a lower court.

arraignment   A legal proceeding in which an accused person is brought before a court to answer a criminal charge.

brief   A document submitted to a court by a lawyer (or other party) that outlines the legal arguments in a case.

capital   Involving, potentially, the death penalty.

certiorari   A formal order by a higher court requiring the lower court to send it the records of a case for review.

common law   The laws originating from long-standing customs rather than from written statutes.

cross-examine   To question a witness in a court case, by the lawyer of the opposing side.

docket   The list of cases to be tried by a court.

due process (of law)   The procedures in the administration of justice that respect the rights of individuals.

equal protection (of law)   The right of each citizen to enjoy the same rights as everyone else.

federalism   The relationship between the powers of the U.S. government and the powers of governments of the 50 states.

felonies   Major crimes, such as robbery or murder, that may be punishable by confinement in a state or federal prison.

habeas corpus   A court order to release a prisoner being held in custody.

incorporate   The legal doctrine that allows a part of the Bill of Rights to be applied to the states through the due process clause of the Fourteenth Amendment.

indigent   Poor.

in forma pauperis   A typed or handwritten petition to the Supreme Court to waive the filing fees of an appeal.

jurisdiction   A court's power and right to hear a case.

misdemeanors   Minor crimes, less serious than felonies, that result in fines or confinement in a county jail.

petition   A formal, written request to a court.

plea bargain   Negotiations between the prosecutor and an accused to avoid a trial; as a result, the accused admits to the crime (or a lesser offense) in exchange for a lighter sentence.

prosecutor   The lawyer who represents the government in a trial.

Supreme Court   The highest court in the United States, the decisions of which are binding on all other courts in the country.

waive   To voluntarily give up of a right or benefit.

Bibliography

Banaszak, Ronald, Sr. *Fair Trial Rights of the Accused: A Documentary History.* Westport, Conn.: Greenwood, 2002.

Barker, Lucius, et al. *Civil Liberties and the Constitution.* 9th ed. Englewood Cliffs, N.J.: Prentice Hall, 2004.

Beany, William Merritt. *The Right to Counsel in American Courts.* Ann Arbor: University of Michigan Press, 1955.

Irons, Peter, and Stephanie Guitton, eds. *May It Please the Court.* New York: New Press, 1993.

Lewis, Anthony. *Gideon's Trumpet.* New York: Random House, 1964.

National Symposium on Criminal Defense. *Improving Criminal Justice Systems Through Expanded Strategies and Innovative Collaborations.* Washington, D.C.: Government Printing Office, 2000.

Nowak, John E., and Ronald D. Rotunda. *Constitutional Law.* 7th ed. Hornbook Series. Eagan, Minn.: West Group, 2004.

Taylor, John B. *The Right to Counsel and Privilege Against Self-Incrimination.* Santa Barbara, Calif.: ABC-Clio, 2004.

Further Reading

Banaszak, Ronald, Sr. *Fair Trial Rights of the Accused: A Documentary History.* Westport, Conn.: Greenwood, 2002.

Dudley, Mark. *Gideon v. Wainwright.* New York: Twenty First Century Books, 1997.

Force, Eden. *The Sixth Amendment.* Englewood Cliffs, N.J.: Silver Burdett, 1991.

Lewis, Anthony. *The Supreme Court and How It Works: The Story of the Gideon Case.* New York: Random House, 1966.

Lewis, Anthony, and David W. Rintels. *Gideon's Trumpet.* DVD. Directed by Robert E. Collins. New York: WorldVision, 1998.

Patrick, John J. *The Bill of Rights: A History in Documents.* New York: Oxford University Press, 2003.

Prentzas, G.S. *Miranda Rights: Protecting the Rights of the Accused.* New York: Rosen Publishing Group, 2006.

Taylor, John B. *The Right to Counsel and Privilege Against Self-Incrimination.* Santa Barbara, Calif.: ABC-Clio, 2004.

Wice, Paul. Gideon v. Wainwright *and the Right to Counsel.* Danbury, Conn.: Franklin Watts, 1995.

Organizations

American Civil Liberties Union
125 Broad Street, 18th Floor
New York, NY 10004
212-944-9800
http://www.aclu.org

National Legal Aid & Defenders Association
1140 Connecticut Ave. NW, Suite 900
Washington, DC 20036
202-452-0620
http://www.nlada.org

Supreme Court Historical Society
224 East Capitol St., NE
Washington, D.C. 20543
202-543-0400
http://www.supremecourthistory.org/

Web Sites

A variety of resources on *Gideon* can be found at
    http://www.nacdl.org/Gideon.
Information on *Gideon* and its effect in Florida can be found at
    http://www.rashkind.com/Gideon/florida_bar_journa.htm.
Information on *Gideon* and other landmark Supreme Court cases
    can be found at http://www.landmarkcases.org/.
Information on the Scottsboro Boys case can be found at http://
    www.pbs.org/wgbh/amex/scottsboro/.
Information on the Sixth Amendment can be found at http://
    supreme.lp.findlaw.com/constitution/amendment06/index.html.
Information on the Supreme Court can be found at http://
    www.supremecourtus.gov/.
National Symposium on Criminal Defense's *Improving Criminal
    Justice Systems Through Expanded Strategies and Innovative
    Collaborations* can be found at http://www.ojp.usdoj.gov/
    indigentdefense/icjs.pdf.
Oral arguments for *Gideon v. Wainwright* can heard at
    http://www.oyez.com/oyez/resource/case/139/audioresources.
The U.S. Constitution can be found at http://www.archives.gov/
    national-archives-experience/charters/constitution.html.
U.S. Supreme Court opinions can be found at http://
    www.findlaw.com/casecode/supreme.html.
U.S. Supreme Court rules can be found at
    http://www.supremecourtus.gov/ctrules/rulesofthecourt.pdf.

EQUAL·JUSTICE·UNDER·LAW·

Picture Credits

Index

About the Author

G. S. Prentzas is an editor and writer who lives in New York. He has written more than a dozen books for young readers, including *Thurgood Marshall: Champion of Justice, Tribal Law,* and *Miranda Rights: Protecting the Rights of the Accused.* He graduated with honors from the University of North Carolina School of Law.

About the Editor

Tim McNeese is an associate professor of history at York College, in York, Nebraska, where he is in his fifteenth year of college instruction. Professor McNeese earned his associate of arts degree from York College, a bachelor of arts in history and political science from Harding University, and a master of arts in history from Southwest Missouri State University. A prolific author of books for elementary, middle, and high school, and college readers, McNeese has published more than 80 books and educational materials over the past 20 years on everything from Mississippi steamboats to Marco Polo. His writing has earned him a citation in the library reference work, *Something About the Author.* Professor McNeese served as a consulting historian for the History Channel program, "Risk Takers, History Makers." Readers are encouraged to contact Professor McNeese at tdmcneese@york.edu.